PASTORS ◆ ◆ ◆ IN MINISTRY

PASTORS IN MINISTRY

Guidelines for Seven Critical Issues

William E. Hulme
Milo L. Brekke
William C. Behrens

AUGSBURG Publishing House • Minneapolis

PASTORS IN MINISTRY
Guidelines for Seven Critical Issues

Copyright © 1985 Augsburg Publishing House

Scripture quotations unless otherwise noted are from the Revised Standard Version of the Bible, copyright 1946, 1952, and 1971 by the Division of Christian Education of the National Council of Churches.

Library of Congress Cataloging in Publication Data

Hulme, William Edward, 1920-
   PASTORS IN MINISTRY.

   1. Pastoral theology.   I. Brekke, Milo L.   II. Behrens,
William C., 1933-   III. Title.
BV4011.H77   1985   253'.2   85-1213
ISBN 0-8066-2159-1

Manufactured in the U.S.A.   APH 10-4898

1   2   3   4   5   6   7   8   9   0   1   2   3   4   5   6   7   8   9

CONTENTS

71333

INTRODUCTION

As a professor of pastoral care and pastoral counseling in a theological seminary, Dr. William Hulme became concerned about the frustrations and lack of fulfillment he was perceiving in the lives of parish pastors, many of them his former students. Since he was aware that counselors tend to generalize on their experience and their experience is primarily with the troubled, he wondered whether the negative impression he was receiving was an accurate assessment of the state of the parish ministry. The question was important to him because he felt a responsibility for the students whom he was helping to educate for this profession. Was the seminary adequately preparing them for the realities of the parish ministry? Or was it setting them up for disillusionment? Since his own son was one of these students, these questions were of personal concern as well.

The Project

How then to determine an accurate picture of the parish ministry? For this he needed an accurate report from clergy of all ages, from all kinds of parishes, and from all parts of the country. The most feasible way to do this seemed to be by questionnaire. He also needed a cross-cultural check in order to ascertain distinctly cultural influences on the American scene. This required a country whose first language was English (to perceive the nuances of the questionnaire) and with a significant Lutheran church body (since the major focus of the study would be with Lutherans). These conditions were best met in Australia, which has only one Lutheran church body that, though small by American measurements, is much more significant in the smaller Australian population, including the proportionately smaller church population. The entire project, including a prospective trip to Australia, became the agenda for a sabbatical leave.

While he had many ideas about what he wanted to find out from parish clergy, he was not equipped educationally or by experience to devise or tabulate such a questionnaire. So he presented his project to the Office of Support to Ministries of The American Lutheran Church and was referred to Dr. William C. Behrens, the director of support systems. Behrens responded positively to the idea and enlisted the assistance of Dr. Milo L. Brekke, whose expertise in the area of the devising and interpreting of questionnaires has been established through his work on studies such as *Ministry in America* and *A Study of Generations*.[1] Brekke also responded positively, and the team was formed.

Brekke began by conducting a search of the literature concerning surveys and other empirical studies of clergy and their families in regard to a number of issues and potentially debilitating influences that Hulme had identified, such as:

- The pastor's experience of pressure for upward mobility and reactions or responses to such pressures.
- The way cultural values, rather than those of the gospel, influence the pastor's and congregation's evaluation and interpretation of the quality of congregational life.
- The way pastor and congregation deal with conflict—in the congregation, within the biological family, with clergy peers, and with denominational officials.

- The effects, if any, of occupational frustration on the clergy marriage and family and vice versa.

- With the heavy demand in the profession for possessing intangibles like faith and love, the role that doubt—over whether one has these qualities—has in the creation of stress and dissatisfaction.

- The role that stress in one's marriage and family has on the pastor's image of himself or herself as qualified for the practice of ministry.

- Whether there is sufficient feedback for the pastor to evaluate his or her ministry or sufficient reinforcement for support in stressful seasons.

As a consequence, many of the items in the resulting questionnaire were, or were based upon, questions used successfully in previous research.

When the questionnaire was prepared, the bishops and district presidents of the American Lutheran Church (ALC), the Lutheran Church in America (LCA), the Lutheran Church–Missouri Synod (LC–MS), the Evangelical Lutheran Church of Canada (ELCC), as well as leaders in some other major denominations, were informed of Hulme's desire to administer the questionnaire at their district conferences or other gatherings and of his availability for programs of pastoral import.

In addition, Hulme arranged with Dr. Les Grope, president of the Evangelical Lutheran Church of Australia, through The American Lutheran Church's Division for World Mission and Inter-Church Cooperation, to come to Australia as their guest as well as program resource for the successively scheduled annual pastoral conventions of the districts of the church. Besides this trip to Australia, Hulme's sabbatical year was composed of some 45 trips to the various synods, districts, and conferences of the Lutheran church bodies of the United States and Canada, during which he personally administered the questionnaire to the clergy and spouses who were present. In addition to these scheduled pastoral conferences, there were also several district clergy/

spouse retreats and two retreats for spouses alone. Pastors attending the Kairos continuing education programs and other clergy gatherings at Luther Northwestern Seminary were also included. In a few situations when Hulme was not able personally to administer the questionnaire to ALC district conferences, he arranged for former students to administer the questionnaire for him. The results of these efforts, extending through 30 months, beginning in February 1982, produced 1,220 usable questionnaires.

How now to have the data processed and analyzed? Behrens approached the Council of Presidents of the ALC to request funds for this program from Aid Association for Lutherans. These were granted and the questionnaires went to the computer.

The Limitations

There are both limitations and strengths in this type of inquiry. First, the limitations.

1. These tabulated questionnaires are not a random sample of clergy and certainly do not represent all clergy of the church bodies involved. Rather, they are confined to the clergy who attended the regularly scheduled synodical or district pastoral conferences and, to a much lesser extent, those who attended district-sponsored retreats and seminary- or hospital-sponsored continuing education programs.

2. There is not an equal or proportionate representation of church bodies or of clergy and spouses. The majority of the questionnaires are from ALC pastors and spouses, with a significant minority coming from LCA and LC–MS pastors and spouses and from the ELCC. Other denominations, and these include most of the major denominations and many of the smaller ones, constitute the smallest proportion. Also, these questionnaires are predominately from clergy, although spouses constitute about 20% of them. With only 32 female clergy represented—which reflects the representation of women clergy at these gatherings—there are

scarcely enough to draw conclusions. What we get about them are clues at best. We will deal with these primarily in Chapter 4. The breakdown of respondents was as follows: 957 male clergy, 209 male-clergy spouses, 11 male clergy who were also female-clergy spouses, 24 female clergy, 9 female-clergy spouses, and 8 female clergy who were also male-clergy spouses. Table 1-1 provides further description of those who answered the questionnaire.

There are, of course, some instances in which both husband and wife from the same marriage were individual respondents, but because some of the retreats were for spouses only, data from the majority of spouses are unmatched with their clergy spouses.

The Strengths

1. Since Hulme was concerned first with his own church body, and since Behrens and Brekke were associated with the administration of that same church body, all of the 19 districts of the ALC are significantly represented. The other two major Lutheran bodies, LCA and LC–MS, have a significant, though less uniform, representation. The ELCC, a smaller body, is well represented, and the ELC of Australia has probably the most thorough coverage of all. With the exception of the Australian church, which was the cross-cultural check, the data revealed very few differences among the clergy of these church bodies as well as with those of other denominations. Although spouses were in the minority, there are sufficient of them from wide enough sources for these data to merit serious attention.

2. There was a good range of age, stages of family life-cycle, marital status, years in the ministry, types of call (team or solo pastoral ministries, institutional chaplains, and church administrators), geographical location, and types of parish (central city, urban, suburban, small town, and rural). Chaplains and church administrators were in sufficient numbers to provide a comparison with parish pastors.

Approximately 65% of the clergy respondents were solo pastors of parishes, 10% were associate or assistant pastors, 10% were senior pastors, 5% were copastors, and 10% are chaplains, administrators, and workers in other specialized ministries. Forty percent of the spouses who responded were employed for pay. Ninety-five percent of the clergy listed themselves as married, while only 5% were listed as never married, separated, divorced, or widowed. The median for years in the ministry of the respondents was 25.

3. In line with proper research procedure, a standardized way of administering the questionnaire was followed. Even on the few occasions when Hulme did not administer the questionnaire, those who did followed a uniform procedure which included the following instructions:

a. You are assured of the anonymity and confidentiality of your responses to the questionnaire.

b. The questionnaire asks for personal information. It is important to obtain this information in order to assist offices for support to ministries as well as theological seminaries to do their task. So we encourage you to share what you really feel and believe.

c. We ask for your candor. Do not try to figure what the questionnaire wants, but rather give immediate responses to the question. Check the first choices that come to mind. Don't ponder—or be particularly cautious.

d. Give only one answer to every question unless instructed otherwise in the questionnaire.

e. Please use the back page for written comments. These are of special value to us.

f. The questionnaire will take about 25 minutes to complete.

4. Hulme interviewed randomly selected former students in depth regarding their assessment of their life in parish ministry as well as receiving their questionnaires. In addition, all of the participants were encouraged to respond to the final question, which requested written comments concerning their views of the

health or unhealth of the parish ministry. The contents from these interviews and written comments were utilized to supplement data from the questionnaire when applicable.

Because of the nature of these limitations and strengths of the study, the authors have not interpreted the data with a strong emphasis on the exact percentages of those who answered in a given way but rather with confidence in the major emphases, consistent differences between groups, and consistent patterns of response.

How to Read and Use the Book

After the myriad pages of computerized summaries of the data were read and analyzed, the authors reflected on these findings and perceived where the major emphases seemed to focus. These then became the topics of the chapters in this book. Each chapter, therefore, reports and describes a major issue, need, or concern of the respondents as identified from the data. We suggest that you read through the questionnaire in Appendix A before you begin the next chapter. This will familiarize you with the descriptive terms used in the data summaries at the beginning of each chapter.

Two Important Distinctions

In order to keep from misunderstanding and misinterpreting data presented throughout the book, it is essential to keep two things straight. The first is the difference between *descriptive* research or analysis and *causative* research or analysis. What are presented in this book are the results of *descriptive* research. No attempt has been made to identify the cause(s) of phenomena that are reported. The difference is between presenting *what* is the case and *why* it is that way. For example, when examining correlations between certain kinds of answers to survey questions and characteristics of different groups of people who answered, one might discover and report that certain beliefs or behaviors are more common among people of higher socioeconomic status who live in suburban settings. That is a description. It does not include any claim that higher socioeconomic level and living in suburbia cause such beliefs or behaviors. With the proper kinds of data and analyses, one might be able to discover that, in point of fact, both the higher socioeconomic level and place of residence are caused by level of education, and that, therefore, educational level is the primary cause of the belief and behavior in question. This book provides *description* of what is more and less characteristic or frequent among certain subgroups of clergy and/or spouses. Those correlations should not be understood or interpreted as *causes*.

The second important distinction is the difference between what is generally characteristic of one or more groups and what is the characteristic difference between two groups. What is characteristic of a group is what is the *most common or frequent* response to a question by people in that group. The characteristic difference between two groups is *what is different about, or distinguishes between*, the answers given to a question by the people in the two groups. To illustrate: suppose that two groups of people both respond to a survey question that allows the answers "frequently," "occasionally," or "never." Suppose that 75% of both groups answer "occasionally." Suppose also that in Group A, 20% answer "frequently" and 5% answer "never." And suppose also that in Group B, 5% answer "frequently" and 20% answer "never." Under such circumstances, the *characteristic* answer of both groups is "occasionally" (the vast majority of both groups answered that way). However, the *characteristic difference* between the two groups is that Group A has a greater tendency to answer "frequently," and Group B has a greater inclination to answer "never." In most of the chapters of the book, two groups are being compared, and the characteristic differences between the two groups are being reported and discussed. It is important that those characteristics that differentiate between the two groups (characteristic differences) *not* be misunderstood and/or misinterpreted as if they were the most common characteristics or responses of either group (what generally characterizes either of them). As in the illustration above, what generally characterizes both groups may be occasional behavior of a certain sort, but what distinguishes between, or is different about, the two groups is that in one group frequent behavior of that sort is more common, while in the other group *never so behaving* is more common. Throughout the book, if two groups are not being compared, then what is generally characteristic is being described. If two groups are being compared, then characteristic differences between the groups are usually being presented.

The Writers

The first part of each chapter dealing with the questionnaire data was written by Brekke. The second part, on reflection and interpretation, was written by Hulme, and the third part, on practical ways for improvement, was written by Behrens. Yet each of these parts was discussed and critiqued in detail by the three authors, who met on a regular basis for this purpose. Since each has his own expertise and perspective, the writing was allotted on this basis, but all are speaking in each of the sections.

This book is for everyone who is interested in the office of parish ministry and in the life and ministry of the parish. This includes especially clergy, spouses, laity of the congregations, denominational officials, and seminary professors and students. It can be read individually and also as a group text for congregational groups, pastoral conferences, denominational executives, and theological professors and students. It is the hope of the authors that the salient findings and implications, as described in the following chapters, will help improve the health of the parish ministry and the lot of the parish pastor and his or her spouse and family.

TABLE 1-1

Distribution of Those Who Answered the Questionnaire

1. Sex and Clergy Status

957　Male clergy
209　Male-clergy spouses
　11　Male clergy who were also female-clergy spouses
　24　Female clergy
　　9　Female-clergy spouses
　　8　Female clergy who were also male-clergy spouses
　　2　Unknown

1220 TOTAL

2. Age

　　7　Age under 26
125　Age 26-30
180　Age 31-35
218　Age 36-40
156　Age 41-45
197　Age 46-50
142　Age 51-55
　90　Age 56-60
　64　Age 61-65
　12　Age 66-70
　11　Age 70+
　18　Age unknown

1220 TOTAL

3a. Church Body

728　American Lutheran Church
　97　Lutheran Church in America
104　Lutheran Church–Missouri Synod
259　Other
　32　Unknown

1220 TOTAL

3b. Church Body (Clergy Only)
- 550 American Lutheran Church
- 85 Lutheran Church in America
- 100 Lutheran Church–Missouri Synod
- 8 Other U.S. Lutheran
- 45 Evangelical Lutheran Church of Canada
- 113 Evangelical Lutheran Church of Australia
- 99 Other denominations

1000 TOTAL

4. Marital Status
- 42 Never married
- 1159 Married
- 3 Separated
- 7 Widowed

1220 TOTAL

5. Family Status
- 40 Not married (or unknown)
- 92 I. Married (no children)
- 61 II. Beginning family (oldest child less than 30 months)
- 102 III. Family with preschool children (oldest 30 months to 6 years)
- 245 IV. Family with school children (oldest 6-13 years)
- 244 V. Family with teenagers (oldest 13-20 or so years)
- 238 VI. Family as launching center (first child gone to last child leaving)
- 173 VII. Family in middle years (empty nest to retirement)
- 25 VIII. Aging family (in retirement)

1220 TOTAL

6. Type of Call
- 730 Solo pastor
- 117 Associate or assistant
- 50 Copastor
- 138 Senior pastor
- 45 Chaplain
- 8 Educator
- 17 Administrator
- 52 Other specialized ministry
- 63 Unknown (mostly spouses)

1220 TOTAL

7. Parish
     837   One congregation
     212   More than one congregation
      10   Agency or institution
     161   Unknown (mostly spouses)
 _____

1220 TOTAL

8. Primary Location
      22   Inner city of metropolis over 1,000,000
      49   Urban area of metropolis
     170   Suburb of metropolis
      29   Center of large city (250,000–1,000,000)
      38   Urban area of large city
      84   Suburb of large city
      42   Center of medium city (50,000–250,000)
      29   Urban area of medium city
      40   Suburb of medium city
     166   Small city (10,000–50,000)
     146   Town (2500–10,000)
     188   Rural town (under 2500)
      87   Rural or farm (open country)
     130   Unknown
 _____

1220 TOTAL

1

Achieving
Competence and Satisfaction
in Ministerial Functions

Data Summary

Lutheran clergy generally feel *most positive* about six ministerial activities, beginning with the highest rated:

- preaching
- worship leading
- teaching of adults
- sick visitation
- ministry with the aged
- counseling

When asked to rate "Activities that I feel positive about in my ministry," they gave average ratings of 4.4 to 3.6 to those six activities on a scale where 5 = most positive and 1 = not positive. It is reasonable to consider those six as an interrelated set of ministerial activities. Apparently they have something in common. Individual pastors consistently tended to rate them as a set about which they feel more positive.

By contrast, they generally feel *least positive* about the following beginning with the least positive:

- youth work
- evangelism
- community responsibilities
- administration
- prophetic witness
- confirmation
- specialized group work

19

On the same scale, they rated these seven activities an average of 3.1 to 3.3. These also apparently have something in common that makes them a set about which Lutheran pastors generally feel less positive.

Pastors' sense of competence about, or satisfaction with their performance of, different aspects of ministry is related to gender, location, denomination, position, and age or stage of family life—but not strikingly so.

Men and women clergy are about equally satisfied with their performance of the various facets of ministry. Pastors serving in urban areas are more satisfied than the average with their specialized group work, while rural pastors are significantly less. But pastors in rural areas are more satisfied with their sick visitation, while suburban pastors are significantly less satisfied than the average pastor with their calling on the sick. Otherwise, pastors serving in different kinds of locations reported no systematic differences in sense of satisfaction.

Differences by denomination were also few. Pastors of the LC–MS generally reported feeling better than LCA pastors about teaching adults, and vice versa about leading worship. ALC pastors felt somewhat more positive than the rest about their prophetic witness.

Assistant and associate pastors report about an average sense of satisfaction across the various aspects of ministry as a whole. However, solo pastors feel somewhat less positive generally than do senior pastors who on the average have the highest general sense of satisfaction of all, particularly concerning the seven activities about which pastors in general feel *least* positive.

Like senior pastors, those whose children are teenage and older, and those who have reached that stage in life without children, generally feel more positive about ministry as a whole. But, by contrast with senior pastors, they report feeling particularly positive about the six activities that ministers in general feel *most* positive about (preaching, teaching, worship leading, sick visitation, work with the elderly, and counseling).

Non-Lutheran clergy who were part of this sample reported significantly greater satisfaction than Lutherans did with counseling (ranked fourth rather than sixth) and evangelism (ranked seventh rather than twelfth). They reported significantly less satisfaction on the average than Lutherans with ministry to the aged (ninth rather than fifth).

Interpretation and Reflections

Division Corresponds to Seminary Curricula

These two sets of ministries with contrasting degrees of satisfaction correspond to contrasting emphases in most seminary curricula. As far as core requirements are concerned, the majority of seminaries are strong on preaching, worship, teaching, sick, shut-in visitation, and often in counseling. By contrast, courses in youth work, evangelism, community responsibilities, administration, and specialized group work—if they exist at all— are usually electives.

It is significant also that senior pastors, who are shown to be most positive and least stressed of all clergy, do not as a rule have as their primary responsibilities those ministries that clergy as a whole tend to feel least positive about. This is of particular interest, since senior clergy contrast with other clergy in feeling more positive about these very ministries. In actuality, these ministries—youth work, evangelism (other than preaching), community responsibilities, specialized group work, and even to some degree confirmation—are assigned to associates as primary responsibilities. The exception is administration.

What seems to result from this differentiation is that the ministries about which clergy as a whole feel least positive and have the least training for are allotted in team ministries to those least experienced and, therefore, most vulnerable. Youth work is a good example. Our seminary interns are most likely to receive the youth group as their assignment; yet they may have had little preparation and experience for this task, which is usually considered to be one of the most frustrating ministries.

While one may be competent in a ministry that one receives little satisfaction from, it is difficult to conceive of feeling positive about a ministry that one feels *incompetent* in. Consequently, there would seem to be a direct relationship between feeling positive about a ministry and feeling competent in that ministry. If, as has been indicated, these ministries about which clergy feel less positive are also those for which they have received the least training, then it is likely that feelings of inadequacy are a primary factor in this dissatisfaction. Therefore, seminary curricula as well as continuing education programs containing courses in the ministries of evangelism, youth work, specialized group work, community responsibilities, administration, and the prophetic witness ought to increase the satisfaction in these ministries.

The Need for Control

In addition to an educational deficiency, these contrasts in satisfaction could be attributed to a personal need for control, which inhibits trust. Preaching and worship leading, particularly in a Lutheran or other traditional church setting, are highly controlled ministries. Not all preachers agree that they have a sense of control in preaching. Some do not feel positive about this ministry. Others who do may feel apprehensive precisely because they feel they lack control. This is due largely to the preacher's inability to control the congregation's response to the sermon and the preacher's need of reassurance. It is also due to the frequent experience of after-the-fact realizations of how one could have done better in preparation or delivery. Some also are frightened by the sheer responsibility, if not audacity, of claiming to preach the Word.

In spite of these nonpredictable aspects of preaching that may cause apprehensions, the fact remains that sermons are prepared and generally preached as the preacher had anticipated. The worship liturgies are normally prescribed and used repeatedly. Congregational interreaction is also somewhat predictable. The preacher—the worship leader—is definitely in more control here than in the ministries of less positive satisfaction. If preachers can control themselves to do their preparation, for example, they are relatively sure when and how they will begin their preaching, where they are going in the process, and how they will finish. They also know that no one is likely to interrupt them or verbally disagree with them while they are preaching or leading worship. Nonverbal communication from the listeners, however, can be quite disconcerting.

Teaching adults and visiting the sick and aged are less predictable but are still largely controlled by the teacher or visitor. The teacher prepares his or her lesson and may or may not save much time for discussion, which would be much less controlled. The sick and the aged are often made passive by their afflictions, even being confined to wheelchairs or hospital beds. The visitor decides when to visit and when to terminate the visit, simply by being ambulatory, if nothing else. Counseling is not controlled to this extent and, therefore, is less predictable, but we will discuss this exception later in the chapter.

In contrast to the preacher, worship leader, and visitor to the sick and aged, the minister in youth work has much less control of the situation. The frequently expressed frustrations in youth ministry are the so-called irresponsibility of youth and the rapid turnover and changing quality of youth leadership. By its aggressive nature, the ministry of evangelism is likely to confront resistance. One can invite and persuade, but the response is highly unpredictable. Specialized group work in which the dynamics of the group are interreactional is again, by its nature, highly unpredictable. The group leader shares control with the others in the group so that the group interreaction itself can be influential.

Prophetic ministry is also in this category but is a story in itself and will be taken up in a later chapter.

Since confirmation is a teaching ministry, it is interesting that it is less satisfying than the teaching ministry to adults. Since both are teaching ministries, the difference must lie in who are being taught. Since confirmation instruction is largely with youth, the diminished satisfaction evidently centers in this factor, since confirmation instruction in many respects is a *youth* ministry.

Possible Interrelationships

These two factors in the discrepancy of satisfaction in the various ministries may well be interrelated. Are we more attracted to ministries in which we can maintain more control, and do we therefore invest more time and energy in them? Could this predisposition even affect the design of seminary and continuing education curricula, or at least the student response to the curricula? On the other hand, may not the inadequacy of training in skills make one feel less secure and less in control in these ministries? In raising these questions, are we asking the perennial question of which comes first, the chicken or the egg, or are both of these factors serving in each capacity? Before answering this question, we need to look more deeply into the effect that this need for control can have on our ministry.

The Higher the Satisfaction the Less the Challenge?

If we are protecting our vulnerability in preferring the more controllable ministries, are we not leaving ourselves unchallenged? In concentrating on these ministries at the expense of the less controllable ones, are we not stifling our personal growth? All of us are sensitive to criticism; some of us protect ourselves from receiving it. The ministries of preaching, worship leading, and adult teaching, for example, rarely provide any overall feedback. By not exposing ourselves to an evaluation, other than on a selective basis, are we defending ourselves against criticism?

As a result, our positive attitude toward these ministries may be lacking to some extent the realism of evaluation. The first test I gave as a college teacher of religion following my ministry in the parish was an eye-opener. It was also unnerving. I couldn't believe the students had comprehended so little of what I was so sure I had communicated so well. The nearest connection to my parish experience was the testing programs in confirmation instruction.

If, on the other hand, one feels positive about the least controllable ministries—where the majority feel least positive—it must indicate another source of satisfaction along with positive feedback. There is an excitement in sharing control. When the outcome is unpredictable the sense of adventure heightens. Since our vulnerability in such sharing is more readily exposed, the potential for growth is enhanced. These exposures, which are more readily defended against in the more predictive ministries, are potential stimuli for growth. They contain the potential for the satisfaction that comes from adventure—from challenge. Tangible results from our ministry, therefore, are not the sole source for satisfaction.

The need for control, which inhibits our involvement in the least controllable ministries, tends to go with a controlling personality. Those of us with this predisposition tend to be overly serious about ourselves and what we do. We work hard as a way of keeping ourselves from being vulnerable. Because of this protective value of work, we tend to become workaholics. This imbalance in work creates all kinds of time pressures. It also leaves us vulnerable to depression if our work fails to give us its promised protection. Criticisms can be devastating when one has worked so hard. Is there no gratitude, let alone commendation, for such "self-giving"?

The imbalance in the life of the controlling person is often revealed by his or her spouse's comment that he or she rarely sees the pastor spouse. This is usually said with a laugh rather than a groan, indicating that the spouse is an enabler of this imbalance. Imbalance in favor of work is obviously the accepted way of qualifying in our culture, because it is a controllable way. One can qualify to some extent, even without achievement, by communicating in one way or another, "Look how hard I'm working!"—a variation of "Look how hard I'm trying!"

The need for control can be a substitute for trust. It seeks to prevent the exposure in which one would have to trust. The contrast is a reflection of the biblical contrast between sight and faith (2 Cor. 5:7). Although "we walk by faith, not by sight," sight provides us more control. Faith means faith in somebody—something—beyond me. With sight I can be more independent. Faith, on the other hand, implies dependency.

The options of independence or dependence imply that it is one or the other. Actually, neither independence nor dependence is the biblical model, but rather interdependence. Faith or trust functions through involvement with others. The paradigm is the human body, whose members are interdependent—each influencing the others and being influenced by them.

The American model or ethos is independence. This is why we are so attracted to independence: it is part of the American spirit. The biblical model has no place for independence: how can one member be independent of the others? The conflict between control and trust is heightened on the American scene by this contrast between "rugged individualism" and biblical corporateness.

In an interdependence model, trusting others is related to trusting oneself, because one is both a receiver and a giver in the mutuality of the body imagery. Perceived within the context of interdependence, vulnerability is not so threatening. I can be trusted to endure, even as I can trust others in my exposure. Inherent in both of these trusts is the basic trust in God. God in Christ is the head of the body, with whom all members are related. Our relationship to ourselves, to God, and other persons is interrelated.

This is illustrated by the two commandments on which "depend all the law and the prophets": "You shall love the Lord your God with all your heart, and with all your soul, and with all your mind," and, "You shall love your neighbor as yourself" (Matt. 22:37-40).

The pains that we seek to avoid by protecting our vulnerability could be the catalyst we need to expand our consciousness and stimulate our personal development. It is not coincidental that a recent study revealed that the clergy who show the most effectiveness and satisfaction in their ministry were those who submitted themselves and their ministry to systematic supervision.[1]

Our choice, then, is to live *defensively*, protecting ourselves from criticism, or to live *offensively*, secure enough to risk exposure. How often have we said or heard it said, "I would rather do it myself. Besides saving myself a lot of time and energy, it would be done right." Regardless of the amount of truth or arrogance in this statement, behind it lies the need to keep control. According to a 1980 study on church growth, "Pastors all too often do not feel confident nor productive in their work unless they are the central doer of ministry."[2]

The choice to live offensively should be understood not as *giving offense* but as *taking the offensive*. Kierkegaard believed a Christian should always be on the offensive; defending is a sign of unbelief: "He who first injected the notion of defending in Christendom is de facto Judas No. 2."[3] Living offensively is actually living out our interdependence according to the biblical model.

The trust inherent in any system in which there is a mutuality of giving and receiving is an obvious catalyst for lay leadership. Comments of the clergy reveal that they feel there is a lack of such leadership. "I envy the local Baptists, who seem to produce leaders that make lay leadership a real vocation," wrote one pastor. "I often wonder why we cannot do the same." This pastor was a Lutheran, and Lutherans have historically given larger authority to clergy than have Baptists.

Besides being a called and ordained minister to others, the pastor is also a called and ordained equipper of lay ministry. Not all congregations want such an equipper, since it puts the responsibility for ministry also on them. Yet, the ministry of the congregation is a shared ministry. The pastor retains control, even as he or she shares it. Clergy are like spiritual midwives in their calling to bring forth, encourage, and educe the priesthood—the pastorhood—of each member of the body.

As clergy, the pastor *has* authority, but in the independence model, he or she uses it as one also *under* authority. This produces a style of leadership that encourages the distribution of power. As priests of God, clergy have the power of a symbolic role to *convince* and *persuade*. Yet, in the mutuality of interdependence, clergy can also *be influenced and persuaded* by others in the body.

To exercise their control in an interdependent community, pastors may need to remove themselves at times from the driver's seat and sit beside the learning driver. While some control is retained, control is also shared. As "new drivers" demonstrate competence, they are given greater responsibility in the ministry of the body.

In spite of the fact that an interdependent leadership style is by its very nature a catalyst for lay ministry, pastors in the survey rated the stimulation of this lay ministry as one of the activities that provides them with the least satisfaction. Does this not correspond with their selection of ministries about which they feel least positive? Is the need to control not only a factor in one's choice of ministries but also in a failure to stimulate lay leadership? While one could conceivably find little satisfaction in an activity in which one is competent, it is difficult to believe this to be the case in an activity as rewarding as stimulating lay leadership. The merger plans of the new Lutheran church combining the ALC, LCA, and AELC are characterized by an increased role for lay leadership. The question is whether either the laity or the clergy is ready for it.

Styles of Leadership

Based on a biblical model of interdependence, the dynamic of trust leads to a particular style of leadership. Like all other groupings, the congregation functions best when it is organized. But how or around what should it be organized? According to the biblical model, the organized focus is the Holy Spirit, the person of the godhead associated directly with the guidance of the church. The pastor and other congregational leaders can and should use tested methods of operation, for example, management by objective. Yet, when used in the body, such a method needs to be "baptized"; that is, the method needs to be viewed as a means by which the Spirit directs the church. The church is an institution like other institutions, but it is also different. In its organizational structure as a body, its central character or focus is God.

The composers of *Jesus Christ Superstar* also composed *Joseph's Technicolor Dream Coat*. It is a lighthearted operetta based on the story of Joseph and his coat of many colors. While the biblical story was central to the operetta, the story's central character was omitted. Although his brothers meant evil against Joseph when they sold him into slavery, in the operetta there is no Yahweh who "meant it for good, to bring it about that many people should be kept alive" (Gen. 50:20). Likewise, it is not uncommon for congregations to function with an organizational plan but without an awareness of the central character of the organization, the Holy Spirit. Although the Holy Spirit uses means, the Spirit is bigger and beyond the means. Because method is not an end in itself, we do not give it ultimate seriousness. Rather, it needs to be integrated into this theocentric base.

The distinctiveness of the biblical perspective is shown in the realization that the Spirit may use even the defeat of an organizational goal. As God's people we are ready to be surprised by grace. Methods as means have a limited but also necessary role. The Holy Spirit is a free Spirit, unlimited, utilizing limited forms, but not bound to any of them. Therefore we are free to select forms, methods, and means, based on the nature of the task and the context within which it is carried out.

Protection against Chaos

The opposite mind-set is rigidity in regard to forms: things must be a certain way. Consequently, one does not recognize values in other ways. This is the difference between an *ideological* approach and a *theological* one. The open mind necessary to recognize the Spirit's central role is not possible without the possibility for a change of mind. When we get locked into means, we lose the open-endedness needed for trust.

Rigidity is a protection against chaos. Chaos is frightening; we prefer order. One way of ensuring this order is to confine ourselves to the "security of the familiar." Then anything that is unfamiliar is instinctively ruled out. When we focus only on the familiar forms, we close our eyes to the larger reality. Perhaps we fear chaos too much. Mao Tse-tung saw it as the doorway to change. "There is great chaos under the sun," he wrote, "everything is beautiful."[4] It was probably this appreciation for chaos that led Mao to instigate the Cultural Revolution. But the changes the Cultural Revolution produced were increased persecution and destruction. Mao, unfortunately, had turned chaos as a means for permitting change into chaos as an end; so chaos led only to more chaos.

An attitude of trust in the midst of chaos is something different from either protecting ourselves from it with rigid forms or believing that chaos in itself will lead to positive changes. In Christian terms, trust stems from the security of a *relationship* rather than of a *procedure*. It provides the assurance of divine care. The Spirit is bigger than our risks. The good news is that God is trustworthy. This trustworthiness centers in the story of God's incarnation in Jesus of Nazareth and is made ours by the Spirit's witness with our spirit in our own life stories. By transferring ultimate control to God, trust paradoxically gives us a sense of control.

Pastors face difficult decisions in their leadership, whether they are motivated primarily by trust or by the need to control. The source for the difference lies in the perspective within which the decision is made. When trust is the predominant factor, the decision is made in dialog with the Spirit as a response to what one perceives at the moment as the Spirit's guidance. Yet this inner dialog needs also outer dialogs with the members of the body to help discern the difference between the Spirit's guidance and one's subjective rationalizations. The consultation of these outer dialogs is an example of the interdependence model in action. A recent study of congregations revealed that the top 300 congregations in rate of growth were those in which the leadership was in such shared control.[5]

Skills and Satisfaction

Having investigated the possible influence of the need to control in the selection between the more and less satisfying ministries, we need now to take another look at seminary education, not only as a contributing factor to the difference but also as a way of changing things. There is abundant evidence that skills foster competence, confidence, and satisfaction. A case in point is pastoral counseling. This ministry rates among the more satisfying, yet it is not one that is either controllable or predictable, because it is dialogical. In any genuine dialog, one must share the control; otherwise it is not a dialog. What, in all likelihood, has made the difference in the case of counseling is the Clinical Pastoral Education (CPE) movement. Prior to this movement, counseling was in low repute among the clergy because, more often than not, it was not counseling but rather a transfer of the ministries of teaching or preaching to the one-to-one relationship.

With CPE, however, a supervised and systematic teaching of pastoral counseling as dialog began. Although it was begun outside the seminaries, this clinical emphasis in the teaching of pastoral care and counseling is now an indigenous part of most seminary curricula. I have been a seminary teacher of pastoral counseling in this clinical dimension since 1955. In my present seminary curricula, there are six core quarter-hours of pastoral care and counseling plus many electives.

Besides the training that goes on in seminaries, the CPE centers—usually hospitals—are training thousands of theological students and clergy every year. Once one feels comfortable in dialogical skills, the ministry of counseling becomes exciting. The very unpredictableness due to the shared control makes the counseling session an adventure. As I understand and teach them, the skills of pastoral counseling are methods that are utilized within the context of trust. The end—or ultimate counselor—is the Spirit.

By the same token, could a systematic and supervised approach to the least satisfying ministries over a period of time produce a similar change? If so, by adopting such an approach, our seminaries and continuing education programs could produce more competent evangelists, youth workers, specialized group leaders, and confirmation instructors. On one occasion I taught an elective in youth ministry and assigned each student to prepare a program for a church youth group. With the cooperation of several churches, the students conducted their programs in an actual church youth group and then received feedback from both the youth and the pastor or youth director of the congregation. Programs similar to student teaching in the schools can be set up with local churches and clergy for theological students who are enrolled in classes in Christian education and confirmation instruction. The result of these and similar involvement-oriented courses could result in a more positive attitude toward these ministries as well as an increased trust level, which would, at the same time, reduce the need for control.

For Your Doing

Individual

1. Which functions of pastoral ministry do you find most and least satisfying? Record your responses on Parts A, B, and C of the *Personal Satisfaction* section of the questionnaire in Appendix A (pp. 165-169), and compare your results with those reported in this chapter. Are yours different from the data summary? If so, how?

2. Who is your supervisor? Is this supervisor appropriate for your position? Does this supervision fit with your concept of ministry? How does your bishop's office provide supervision for you? Is the arrangement satisfactory?

3. How do you as pastor share the ministry with your people? Identify and describe specific behaviors of your ministry in the past week that illustrate your skills for shared ministry.
   a. Empowering people
   b. Applying Bible message to life
   c. Active listening
   d. Articulating with clarity
   e. Sharing leadership and decision making

With Others

1. Share your answers to the *Personal Satisfaction* questions with your associate or support group. Ask for their perceptions of what is most satisfying for you. Is it necessary to consider some changes so that you or others can have more satisfying functions?

2. Ask your staff and/or congregational members to evaluate your ministry. Seek guidance and resources for enabling them to do so from your denominational leaders.

3. Challenge yourself by strengthening your competence in an area of ministry that is less satisfying. Remember: supervised practice with new knowledge brings the greatest learning.

Denominational Leaders

1. Support your clergy by providing honest and descriptive feedback. Provide resources that enhance the communication between pastor and lay leaders.

2. Set an example by engaging in a strong continuing education program for yourself and your staff. Challenge clergy to set growth goals and report the results to your office. This subject will be taken up in Chapter 6 as one of the solutions for the pastor's dilemmas described there.

2

Deepening the
Spiritual/Devotional Life

Data Summary

The majority of Lutheran pastors are dissatisfied with their own spiritual and devotional lives. Exactly half report their spiritual or devotional lives to be a source of somewhat serious stress, with another 5% experiencing very serious stress over them (item 84). Sixty-five percent feel no better than "so-so" about their personal prayer lives, with 21% dissatisfied and 3% very dissatisfied (item 44). Seventy-five percent feel no better than "so-so" about their devotional lives with both family and spouse, with 26–32% dissatisfied and 6–7% very dissatisfied (items 45 and 46). While only 16% come right out and agree that their spiritual lives are in trouble (item 182), 41% report they feel at least somewhat bothered because their spiritual lives are in trouble (item 240). In these matters there are no significant differences in pastors from the three Lutheran church bodies or between men and women clergy.

When asked whether they attributed these dissatisfactions to lack of time, energy, cooperation of others, their own motivation or initiative, or clarity as to what they wanted (items 50–52), by far their most frequent reply was their own lack of either motivation or initiative (55%–64%, depending on the specific question).

Pastors who gave a particular answer to one of the first four items mentioned above (items 44, 45, 46, and 182) tended to give the same kind of answer to the other three. That consistency of response was great enough for formation of a scale from those four items, which was called "Sense of Spiritual Inadequacy." Two extreme groups from among all respondents, the 25% with the greatest and the 25% with the least sense of spiritual/devotional inadequacy, were then identified. Their answers to all the rest of the survey questions were then compared for characteristic differences. The two groups differed systematically in their answers to almost half of all questions.

Those *most dissatisfied* with their spiritual/devotional lives were characteristically younger pastors and chaplains in the earlier to middle stages of family life, from the birth of their first child through the period of having children of school age still living at home. The *satisfied* to *very satisfied*, who had little sense of spiritual inadequacy, were more frequently older clergy in other kinds of ministry than parish or chaplaincy, and in the stages of family life from starting to "empty the nest" to retirement and aging. They did not differ significantly by location either by nation (United States, Canada, or Australia) or urban-rural setting. Nor were non-Lutherans different from Lutherans in level of self-perceived spiritual inadequacy.

The two groups did, however, differ significantly in terms of eight other scales. Those with greater sense of spiritual adequacy expressed greater confidence in their competence for both the more easily controlled and the more unpredictable aspects of ministry described in the preceding chapter. They also reported greater general satisfaction with their own accomplishments and self-development, with their relationships with their congregations and spouses, and with contemporary parish ministry as a whole. At the same time, however, they showed more awareness of conflict between Christian values and those of society. By contrast, the group with less sense of spiritual adequacy reported on the average higher levels of stress in two areas: family life and living up to expected roles, including their calling as ministers of the gospel.

Sense of Competence in Ministry

Those dissatisfied with their spiritual/devotional lives were more likely to "tend to disagree" or to "tend to agree" that they like their work, and definitely to agree that they wish they were more efficient in their work and that they often feel everything they do is an effort. They also reported that they were "somewhat" to "quite" bothered by the fact that they felt that way. Conversely, those more satisfied with their spiritual and devotional lives were more likely strongly to agree that they like their work (and yet, strangely, they were more likely to be "very bothered" or "never bothered" by that). They tended definitely to disagree that they wish they were more efficient and that everything they do is an effort (and they were more likely to report never being bothered by that).

Those dissatisfied with their spiritual/devotional lives also more frequently reported being bothered "some" or "very much" by self-doubts about their competency for ministry, and feeling "very dissatisfied" to "so-so" about their sense of doing something of value, their use of their talents, and their general competence in work. Those generally satisfied with their spiritual and devotional lives were much more likely to report being "satisfied" and "never" being bothered by such self-doubts.

Those who perceived themselves as less spiritually adequate were also less inclined to be satisfied with their performance of both of the groups of ministerial activities described in Chapter 1.

Of the more predictable activities they were more likely to feel "positive" about their preaching, "so-so" about their sick visitation, and less satisfied than even "so-so" about their work with the aging. The contrasting group of pastors were more likely to feel "most positive" about all three activities.

Of the less predictable ministerial activities those who perceived themselves as spiritually inadequate were more likely to feel "so-so" or worse about confirmation instruction, and worse than "so-so" about community responsibilities, prophetic witness, youth work, and evangelism—in contrast to the spiritually more satisfied group, which was more likely to feel "positive" to "most positive" about all of these same ministries.

The two groups showed no differences in the patterns of their personal satisfaction from counseling, teaching adults, administration, worship leading, or specialized group work.

General Satisfaction

The pattern of contrasts in general satisfaction with life between those with *great* versus *little dissatisfaction* with their spiritual/ devotional lives is shown in Table 2-1 (p. 39).

The pattern of differences in personal concern between the same two groups is generally one of a tendency to be somewhat to very much bothered versus never or no longer bothered about all of the first set of general satisfactions/dissatisfactions listed above. For example, the group with great sense of spiritual inadequacy was more likely not only to be somewhat to very much bothered by feeling that their lives are not exciting and full of fun and also by feeling that they cannot live up to the standards they set for themselves.

Relationship with the Congregation

While the two groups did not differ in the amount of stress they experienced from conflict with their congregations or unfair treatment from parishioners, the spiritually dissatisfied were more likely to feel dissatisfied with support they receive from their congregations, to experience some to serious stress about income, to be convinced that higher salaries would improve the lot of clergy, to be quite or very bothered by not having enough income

Table 2-1

More frequent response of those with *great dissatisfaction* with their spiritual/devotional lives	Issue	More frequent response of those with *little dissatisfaction* with their spiritual/devotional lives
Tend to disagree or tend to agree	"I find life exciting and full of fun."	Agree or strongly agree
Tend to disagree or tend to agree	"I feel my future is bright."	Agree or strongly agree
Tend to disagree	"I can turn people down, say no, or otherwise decline others in giving priority to my own needs, without feeling guilty."	Tend to agree, agree, or strongly agree
Tend to disagree, disagree, or strongly disagree	"Most of the time I am free of tension and frustration."	Tend to agree, agree, or strongly agree
Agree or strongly agree	"My feelings are easily hurt."	Disagree or strongly disagree
Tend to agree, agree, or strongly agree	"I cannot live up to the standards I set for myself."	Disagree or strongly disagree
Tend to agree, agree, or strongly agree	"I feel angry, frustrated, or tense far too much of the time."	Disagree or strongly disagree
Tend to agree, agree, or strongly agree	"My life-style makes me a high risk for a heart attack."	Disagree

to make ends meet, to feel "so-so" to "dissatisfied," and to experience some to serious stress from perceived lack of freedom to carry out ministry as they understand it. They also were more likely to feel "so-so" to "dissatisfied" with recognition they receive from officers of the congregation and district.

Table 2-2 (p. 40) shows another part of the pattern of differences between the same groups.

Table 2-2

More frequent response of those with *great dissatisfaction* with their spiritual/devotional lives	Issue	More frequent response of those with *little dissatisfaction* with their spiritual/devotional lives
Tend to agree, agree, or strongly agree	"I do not feel good about the appearance of my body."	Tend to disagree, disagree, or strongly disagree
Very dissatisfied to dissatisfied	Distribution of my own time and energy	Satisfied to very satisfied
Very dissatisfied to dissatisfied	Opportunity for balanced living, including time for myself	Satisfied to very satisfied
Very serious stress	Income	No stress
Very serious stress	Time pressures	No stress
Very serious stress	Privacy needs	No stress
Very serious stress	Loneliness/isolation	No stress
Occasionally to frequently	Thoughts of suicide	Never
Occasionally to frequently	Thoughts of self-sabotaging behavior	Never
Occasionally to frequently	Actual self-sabotaging behavior	Never
Somewhat to very bothered	"I get into moods where I can't seem to cheer up."	Never, no longer, or little bothered

By contrast, the group with little sense of spiritual inadequacy was more likely to feel satisfied to very satisfied, to be never or no longer bothered, and to experience no stress concerning all of these matters. They also more frequently reported being very satisfied with the respect and status they receive in the community.

For a personal problem, those less spiritually satisfied claimed they would seek help first from someone *outside* the congregation, while that would be the third or later choice of those more spiritually satisfied.

Sense of Value Conflict

While the spiritually dissatisfied were more inclined to agree strongly with the idea that societal values rather than the gospel seem to influence congregations' evaluations of pastors, those with little dissatisfaction about their spiritual and devotional lives were more likely to disagree. Also, the first group was more likely to report feeling somewhat or quite bothered by being frequently torn by conflicting values, desires, and beliefs *in general*, while the second group was more likely to report "never" or "no longer."

Family

The general pattern of contrast concerning family between those with great versus little dissatisfaction with their spiritual/devotional lives is shown in Table 2-3.

Table 2-3

More frequent response of those with *great dissatisfaction* with their spiritual/devotional lives	Issue	More frequent response of those with *little dissatisfaction* with their spiritual/devotional lives
So-so to dissatisfied	Spouse's close identification with pastor's work	Very satisfied
Very serious stress	Lack of employment opportunities for spouse	No stress
Very serious stress	Conflict with spouse	No stress
Very serious stress	Conflict with own children	No stress
Frequently	Thoughts of giving one's family the "silent treatment"	Never
Frequently	Actually giving one's family the "silent treatment"	Never

Recommend to improve clergy's lot	Provide clergy family retreats and workshops	Not recommend
Recommend to improve clergy's lot	Train Ministerial Relations Committees to work with clergy and their spouses	Not recommend
Recommend to improve clergy's lot	Provide counseling for clergy families	Not recommend
Agree, tend to agree, or tend to disagree, and somewhat to very bothered by it	"Stress in my marriage affects my ministry adversely—makes me feel inadequate in my ministry."	Strongly disagree or disagree, and never or no longer bothered by it
Tend to agree, agree, or tend to disagree, and somewhat to very bothered by it	"The quality of our marriage and family life (were it known) provides poor witness to the congregation and community."	Strongly disagree, and never or no longer bothered by it
Strongly agree, and somewhat to very bothered by it	"I feel I cannot cope with my children."	Disagree, and never or no longer bothered by it
Tend to agree, agree, or strongly agree, and somewhat to very bothered by it	"I feel guilt and disappointment over my performance as a parent."	Disagree or strongly disagree, and never or no longer bothered by it
Tend to agree, agree, or tend to disagree, and somewhat to very bothered by it	"I can't communicate with my spouse."	Disagree or strongly disagree, and never or no longer bothered by it
Tend to agree, agree, or strongly agree, and somewhat to very bothered by it	"My spouse is not as sexually interested in me as I would like."	Disagree or strongly disagree, and never or no longer bothered by it
Tend to agree, agree, or strongly agree, and somewhat to very bothered by it	"I wonder whether my sexual desires are normal."	Disagree, and never or no longer bothered by it
Somewhat to very bothered	"Husbands and wives should share responsibility for household duties."	Little bothered

Living up to Expectations

Very serious stress over "role expectations of self and others" and "frustration in conforming to expectations" is more common among pastors with a greater sense of spiritual inadequacy. They also more often perceive themselves as too anxious to please others, and more often are somewhat bothered by feeling they take their work too seriously and by not being able to sleep before difficult days because they are too anxious. "No stress" and "never" or "no longer bothered" is the more characteristic report from those with little sense of spiritual inadequacy.

Those who view their spiritual/devotional lives with great dissatisfaction also tend more frequently to agree or strongly agree with the statements, "I am inclined to put off dealing with irritations and conflict," and, "I find it very difficult to speak on social issues because of the possible controversy." Members of the other group tend to respond more frequently to those statements with "strongly disagree" or "disagree."

Calling

The group with greater sense of spiritual inadequacy were much more likely to feel "so-so" to "very dissatisfied" about the following: satisfaction with their own ministry, freedom to carry out ministry as they understand it, sense of God's direction in their work, faithfulness to their sense of calling, and relationships with staff and professional co-workers. Those with little sense of spiritual inadequacy were more likely to feel very satisfied or, at least, satisfied.

Those with greater sense of spiritual inadequacy were also more likely to agree with the statements, "I feel inadequate or even hypocritical in being a pastor," and, "I feel uncomfortable about compromises I have made with my calling as God's spokesperson." They were more likely to agree or either "tend to agree" or "tend to disagree" with the statements, "I have self-doubts about my competence in ministry," and, "I often think I could serve God better outside parish ministry." The other group was more likely to respond to those same statements with the opposite. Concerning how they felt about this situation, the two groups again contrasted sharply, with the dissatisfied group more frequently reporting being some to very much bothered, and the other group more frequently reporting never or no longer being bothered.

When asked the reason for their dissatisfaction with their faithfulness to their calling, and with their own ministry, those who perceived their spiritual/devotional lives as inadequate were more likely to answer "lack of clarity as to what I want," in contrast to "lack of time" or "lack of energy" from the other group. When asked about reasons for their dissatisfaction with their prayer and devotional life, the same two groups contrasted again by more frequently answering respectively "lack of own initiative" versus "lack of time or energy."

Interpretation and Reflections

To sum up the findings regarding satisfaction/dissatisfaction with spiritual devotion:

1. A proportionately large number of clergy feel only so-so or dissatisfied about their prayer and devotional life. This includes their personal devotional life, their devotions with spouse, and their family devotions.
2. They account for this dissatisfaction largely by the lack of motivation.
3. Those dissatisfied tend also to feel dissatisfied in their marital and family life, their ministry, with the support from the congregation, and with the attitude of congregational and denominational leaders toward them.
4. They also tend to feel dissatisfied in both sets of ministries described in Chapter 1.

By contrast, those clergy feeling satisfied with their prayer and devotional life tend also to feel satisfied with their marital and family life, their ministry, with the support from the congregation, and with the respect shown them by congregational and denominational leaders. They also feel satisfied in both the predictable and unpredictable ministries.

It would be unwarranted to conclude that the dissatisfaction or satisfaction with one's prayer and devotional life is the basis for the dissatisfaction or satisfaction in these other areas. What we have here is not necessarily a cause-and-effect relationship but rather an aggregate of dissatisfactions or satisfactions, which for some reason seem to go together. Could the differences described simply be the difference between negatively and positively minded people? Or do they reflect the differences between those who face reality and are therefore dissatisfied and those who are satisfied because they deny reality?

Each of these interpretations of the data is possible. It could be that discontent and dissatisfaction in these other areas of the clergy's life may lead to a crisis also in prayer and devotional life. A more likely explanation is that the quality of the clergy's prayer and devotional life has its effect on other aspects of the clergy's life and ministry.

An interesting sidelight in the study is that those who are dissatisfied with their devotional life tend to see the answers to their other dissatisfactions in changes outside of themselves. They believe, for example, that if they had more freedom in which to conduct their ministry, larger salaries, and more recognition from their church and denominations, things would go better in their ministry. By contrast again, those satisfied tend *not* to see these external factors as sources for whatever problems they have. So we raise again the question: Is one's way of interpreting life situations influenced by the quality of one's prayer and devotional life?

The Life-Stage Factor

There is a life-stage factor also involved in this dissatisfaction. The dissatisfied are more likely to be the younger clergy with children at home, while the older clergy whose children are grown are more likely to be satisfied with their devotional life. The life stage probably contributes to this difference. As Urban Holmes puts it, "When we reach the noon of life, the movement is toward the twilight; there is a turning inward."[1] Aging is a spiritual journey. Parental responsibilities are largely in the past for older clergy. There is less pressure to prove oneself as a person or as a pastor; at the same time, one's stage in life moves one to a value system that includes death. For these and other reasons, the spiritual dimension seems to come more into focus in the aging process.

However, should the dissatisfaction with prayer and devotion not resolve itself in the aging process, it could become a provocative factor for a mid-life crisis. Mid-life can be a troublesome time for some people precisely because of unfulfilled dreams. Particularly in the currently "tight" call situation in many churches, some clergy are experiencing frustration over the inability to move. As one such pastor said to me, "Some of us are finding it hard not to become bitter as we are forced to readjust our dreams." The occupational world has a built-in need for upward mobility, and this extends also to clergy.

In such dark times one may wonder about one's calling and about divine providence. The crisis is one of meaning and can leave one's energy depleted. I have talked with several clergy wives concerned about the change that has taken place in their mid-life husbands. The former "go-getter" has become listless. He seems to have lost interest in his work and has little motivation to carry on. What is more frustrating to the spouse is that he won't talk about it. His only way of coping seems to be withdrawal. When I ask, "Do you suppose he is disappointed in what he has achieved in his ministry?" the spouse usually says, "I think he is.'' While there are no guarantees or panaceas, it would seem wise for younger clergy who are dissatisfied with their devotional life to do something about it—if for no other reason than as an investment for a healthy transition from the first to the second half of life.

Priestly Role Threatened

A pastor is a mediator between the world of sense, time, and space and the world of the Spirit, in which tangible measurements do not apply. In this sense, all clergy—regardless of what their denomination may call them—serve a priestly function. While there is one mediator between the people and God, the man Christ Jesus (1 Tim. 2:5), we who are members of Christ's body, the church, continue his mediation. Christ's mediation is incarnational; he makes tangible through his humanity the intangible nature of divinity. Christ's mediation is also reconciliatory; through his death and resurrection he brings forgiveness for our sins. The church carries out these mediatorial functions of Christ, and those ordained by the church and called by the Spirit as clergy carry a special symbolic role in this respect.

The laity look to the clergy for this spiritual leadership—and rightly so—because the spiritual/devotional focus is indigenous to the symbolic role of the ordained. As a clinical psychologist who has related many years with clergy in the clinical pastoral education programs at the Menninger Clinic, Paul Pruyser laments that clergy tend to become psychologists and therapists rather than pastors, although it is precisely for their pastoral position that people come to them in their needs. ''Their [religious] beliefs drive them into the study of their pastor . . . they want their tradition to speak to them.''[2] Pruyser goes on to say that not only should pastoral counseling use religious resources in its healing but also in its diagnostic function. Diagnostic variables peculiar to the religious tradition are the assessment of people's awareness of the holy, their concept of providence, the functioning of their faith, and their receptivity to grace. Such diagnostic variables are unique to the religious tradition and, therefore, to the one bearing the tradition's symbolic role. Therefore, clergy dissatisfaction with their prayer and devotional life is reason for concern, since it is probably a reflection of dissatisfaction with their priestly role.

We find this same dissatisfaction among students in theological seminaries. When I ask my classes how many feel good about their devotional practices, only 10–20% raise their hands. Their faces show the look of concern, and they want to talk about it. It is difficult, they say, to be personal in their religion when they are engrossed with religion in an academic format. Specifically, it is difficult to use the Bible devotionally when it is continually being used as an object of critical study, of hermeneutics, of sermonizing. In this setting the theological concept of the Holy Spirit speaking to our spirits through the Word becomes highly abstract. This same abstraction of the personal dimension of religion may continue in the pastorate, where one's profession is religion.

Another possible cause for the dissatisfaction with devotional life may be the shift that has taken place in the clergy role from *priest of the people* to *executive director of the parish*. Executive directors need organizational ability, persuasive skills, sensitivity to the feelings of others, and a combination of vision and ambition. These are the qualities also needed for successful leadership in other public and private institutions. Yet it is the role of the priest that is unique to spiritual leadership. Instead of being described in this uniquely priestly leadership, clergy are often described in terms of their executive qualities.

In defense of these dissatisfied clergy, it must be admitted that they have not received much reinforcement for their priestly role from our secularized society and even from the congregation, the denomination, or the theological seminary. Our standards of measurement and evaluation for our religious institutions are similar to those of other institutions in our society. Yet clergy themselves tend to see things otherwise. *Growth in Ministry* shows this same dissatisfaction of clergy with their devotional practice, but this is largely because they rate these practices as very important.[3] Out of a possible five points, spiritual development is rated 4.1, the second highest rating of the study. At the same time these clergy rated their effectiveness in their own spiritual development, as well as in their ministry to others, at 3.2, the largest gap between values and fulfillment in the study.

Since clergy as priests are mediators between the world of the Spirit and the world of sensory perception and measurement, there is nothing wrong in being executive directors of the congregation. Congregations obviously function better when they are organized rather than disorganized. When the emphasis is on this phase, however, the other may be neglected. In the subsequent imbalance, the executive director role is a distortion of clergy, because there is no mediation. In this situation the church easily becomes acculturated and loses its distinctive witness.

It takes a priest to be a prophet. The perspective that comes from a spiritual focus sharpens our awareness of the tension between the values of our culture and those of the world of the Spirit. When the executive director role of the clergy is enlarged at the expense of priestly mediation, the congregational activities will become increasingly secularized at the expense of the prophetic witness.

Because of our cultural imbalance in the direction of the tangible, the sensory, the technological, and the material, people have been longing for a restoration of balance—even though they may not have been aware of it. The phenomenal response to the meditative practices associated with Eastern religions is an example of this longing. The response of Christians—who share in this longing—to the writings of Henri Nouwen is another. Clergy and laity of all denominations are attracted to his theological perspective, which is heavily influenced by Catholic spirituality.[4]

A smaller but yet remarkable response to the Quaker emphasis of Richard Foster is another example.[5] Foster's emphasis on the spiritual disciplines is obviously what many Christians have been waiting for.

Lack of Motivation

The disturbing factor in dealing with this clergy dissatisfaction with their prayer and devotional life is that they themselves give *lack of motivation* as the principal reason for their dissatisfaction. What is behind this lack of motivation? The *Growth in Ministry* study indicates that it is not a low priority. Perhaps then it is fear—fear of the unknown, of failure, of the potential chaos that one might confront within oneself should one turn inward. Perhaps also there is confusion over how and where to begin. This seems to be borne out by the reason given by these same pastors concerning their dissatisfaction also with their ministry and their faithfulness to their sense of calling—namely, "lack of clarity of what I want."

Those who are satisfied with their devotional life and their ministry and their faithfulness to their sense of calling give "lack of time and energy" as reasons why they are not more satisfied. These are "creaturely complaints," frustrations over the limits of being limited persons. In contrast, the dissatisfied give an "identity complaint." When we lack clarity over what we want, we are questioning our identity. Since one's calling provides identity, dissatisfaction with faithfulness to this calling could mean lack of clarity concerning the calling. Lack of motivation, therefore, could be carrying the weight of an identity problem.

Ministry of Presence

Prayer and devotional life turn us inward, yet this inward turn is avoided in our secularized pursuits. The pace of an executive director of an organization, including the organization of the parish, may leave little time for reflection. At a meeting of the

American Association of Pastoral Counselors I sat next to a pastor who had recently left the parish ministry to become a full-time pastoral counselor. "It's like I'm out of prison," he said. "I have freedom now just to be, and I am getting to know who I am." I would like to think this can happen within the parish ministry as well as outside of it.

Busyness has long been a protection against getting to know ourselves. We need such protection because we are not sure if we can handle the inward trip. For this we need the courage of faith. As Kierkegaard has pointed out, the more we get into ourselves, the more we see what is frightening and condemning; yet, if we persist, we will also see the outstretched arms of God. It is toward those arms—the promises of his unconditional acceptance—that we take our leap of faith. As priests take this leap and learn to feel at home with themselves in spite of the chaos, they can lead others to cultivate rather than bypass their relationship to themselves.

It is in the balance of the inner with the outer that we can understand and appreciate a ministry of presence. In our cultural values, we are justified by our *doing*. *Doing* is important also in the Christian perspective, but it grows out of and does not substitute for *being*. Our basic gift—like God's—is the gift of ourselves, our person. In our culture persons are what they do. We don't know what to do with a "naked" person. It takes the priestly balance to perceive the person as sufficient in being. A ministry of presence is the gift of one's person—providing comfort in the depths often unreached by actions alone. Other forms of ministry—like other gifts—stem from this giving of one's self, one's ministry of presence.

Making Changes

If you are one of those who feels so-so or even dissatisfied with your devotional life—and what has been said has strengthened your motivation for change—there are things you can do to improve the situation. Of course, there are risks in taking these steps. Some of us are afraid of silence, and these suggestions will take you there. Others will find it hard to change their predisposition to activity, when these steps, in one sense, involve a ceasing of activity. Still others are chary about listening when alone—listening to what, to whom? This may activate our latent doubts about whether anyone is there.

Yet, there are risks also in staying the way we are. The spiritual potential that is ours, both as believers and as priests, may remain undeveloped. We may also continue in bondage to the busyness of our culture, looking always to a nebulous future for our emancipation. These risks are also frightening. So the choice is not between risk and no risk, but of which risks we choose to take.

Alone in God's presence, we can let God's grace justify our existence as well as our ministry, rather than continuing the never-ending attempts to justify ourselves by our busyness, our doing. In God's presence, there is nothing to prove or to accomplish; we can learn from God simply to be. As we develop an at-homeness with ourself alone in the presence of God, we will receive from this experience the spiritual awareness that will enrich all functions of our ministry.

If you are feeling only so-so or dissatisfied about your prayer and devotional life, the first step toward change is seriously to question whether you should continue your present devotional patterns. These now carry with them the onus of indifference or even frustration. If you are like many of us, allotting time for prayer and devotions is adding one more thing to do in a day that is already overly filled with things to do. It then simply adds to the pressure. If you would like to try something different in your devotional life, the following description is one such possibility.

The change I am describing will be a radical one for some of us: to take time to *not* do, rather than to do. This defies all the cultural pressures on us to accomplish something. Rather, we are taking time to do nothing. Just be by yourself and learn to enjoy your own company. You may want to let your mind go back and relive warm and pleasant memories, or you may just let your mind go blank. The main thing is, don't work on anything. Be quiet within. "In quietness and in trust shall be your strength" (Isa. 30:15).

You may find it helpful in slowing the frenetic pace of your mind consciously to relax your body. Begin with your toes and then move to your leg muscles and back muscles to your shoulders. Then go to your fingers and move to your forearm and upper arm muscles and to your facial muscles. As you move through your body in this way, "see" your muscles relaxing. Muscles are fibers sheathed together; visualize these fibers and then tell them to let go, be loose. As you relax your body in this manner, you will feel relaxed also in your mind. It may take several weeks of such daily quieting to reach a relaxed state of body and mind. Persist; it will come.

As you develop this sense of quiet within, you are ready for listening. Listen first to your own inner voice. What are you saying to yourself in your soul? Then listen to the voice of God. In the Christian tradition, it is the Word through which God speaks. Select verses, stories, parables from Scripture that speak especially to you. Memorize the verses, visualize the stories and parables, so that your mind can focus on them at these times. Listen to the Spirit speak through God's Word to you. This is essentially what is described as *meditation* in the Christian perspective. Silence is then listening, receiving. It helps, if feasible, to close your eyes so that you can focus with less distraction on the inner dialog. Use a timer, which will relieve you of concerns about time. When the timer rings, your devotional period is over, regardless of where you are. Listening is not a matter of "getting something done."

Listening to the Spirit *is* prayer. If prayer is conversation with God, then listening to God is an essential part of this conversation.

Our responses to the Spirit's speaking complete the conversational dialog.

In meditation one prays with mental pictures. Our words are symbols of pictures in our mind. As we speak, we stimulate similiar pictures in our hearer's mind—if we are communicating. But God does not need the symbol, because God is aware of the picture. We use words in prayer because we are accustomed to communicating with words, and it heightens our sense of involvement. At times we may want to pray out loud or to express our feelings in tears or with volume, but this is for our benefit and not God's. We should feel free to break out into words whenever we desire.

Praying with pictures fits the highly visual activity of meditation. As you pray for yourself, for your troubled people, for your family, "see" these persons in their needs and feel your compassion for them. Then picture them—yourself, your people, your family—healed, whatever healing may mean in their situation. Take the leap of faith and see it, for seeing is the first step in anticipation.

Your motivation for enhancing your prayer and devotional life will increase as you begin to see—to experience. The value of this time alone with yourself and God, your sense of receiving, of entering into the depths of your soul, and there dialoging with the "Spirit which dwells in you" (Rom. 8:11) helps to shape your perspective. You will begin to see that you owe it to yourself to protect this time—not in obedience to a law so that you won't feel guilty or to bow to the pressure to live up to a clergy image, but rather as a way of enriching your life and the lives of those to whom you are called to minister. It is a way of confirming your call and election (2 Peter 1:10).

These suggestions for developing your prayer and devotional life describe one way of doing it: combining the old practice of daily devotions with the new emphasis on meditation. It is a way I have found helpful. After the death of my daughter over a decade ago, I realized that my old way of devotions was no longer what I needed. This had been largely a focus on Bible study and was now much too cerebral for my *total person* needs.

There are other ways. Some, for example, find satisfaction in the liturgical forms of matins, vespers, compline, or suffrages contained in worship books such as the *Lutheran Book of Worship* or the Episcopal *Book of Common Prayer.*

In the questionnaire clergy dissatisfaction with personal prayer and devotional life extends equally to devotions with spouse and to family devotions. While the place to begin is with ourselves, there is no automatic carry-over to these other devotional groupings. These involve others besides ourselves, and each has its own distinct interpersonal system. In fact, our own devotional life can cause others to feel shut out from this part of our life, if we are praying and meditating when we are obviously needed for other opportunities in our family relationships.

However, since these three dissatisfactions went together, changing one of them may influence the others positively if these dissatisfactions have mutually influenced each other. It is best, though, to talk with our spouse and family members about the situation, sharing our own hopes and desires for these times. It could be that our growing satisfaction with our personal devotional life would incline us to be more positive as well as responsible in our approach to these other devotional opportunities. We are also likely to offer more helpful suggestions. In the next chapter, we will focus on these family relationships.

For Your Doing

Individual

1. What are the satisfactions and dissatisfactions in your spiritual life? Record your responses on parts B-1 and B-2 on the questionnaire (Appendix A) and compare your results with those reported here. How do you resemble the data summary?

2. Take a sheet of paper and in separate columns record the situations in your life over which you have significant influence and those over which you have little or no influence. Note those over which you have little influence and reflect how your devotional life could give you a greater sense of security in these instances.

3. Change your current spiritual disciplines to utilize underdeveloped devotional skills or discover new avenues for your spiritual renewal.

With Others

1. Seek out a spiritual mentor or director. Set some goals, meet monthly, and continue with your director for one year.

2. Briefly write down the dreams you had as a youth and compare them with your life situation today. Have they been realized? Develop some new dreams. Seek out a church career center or a person whose wisdom you respect to help you focus the new dreams.

3. Establish a support group for your personal or professional life. This group should function basically as your "pastor" and provide a "ministry of presence" for you. Check Chapter 6 for ideas on how to establish a support group.

Denominational Leaders and Theological Professors

1. What are the primary roles for which you are preparing clergy? How do you equip pastors for the priestly role as well as preaching? How can you assist pastors in spiritual renewal?

2. Encourage your seminarians to seek out a spiritual counselor for support and spiritual enrichment. Suggest they seek these out within and outside the seminary.

3. Share your spiritual journey with your pastoral colleagues as a means of building community and understanding. Secure for yourself a spiritual counselor.

3

Developing the Potential
of Clergy Marriages

Data Summary

Some clergy came with their spouses to some of the pastoral conferences and retreats where these data were collected. Some clergy came alone without their spouses, and in clergy-spouse conferences, of course only spouses were present. The data reported in this chapter are from *all clergy participants as a whole by comparison with all spouse participants as a whole.* Because most spouses came from the ALC, the possible effect of different proportions of each coming from different Lutheran church bodies was removed statistically. No significant differences were found between the two groups by family life stage, type of pastorate, single congregation or multiple point parish, rural or suburban or urban location, or whether the spouse was employed and the degree of the spouse's satisfaction with that employment. One significant difference was found, however. Matched pairs (a clergy person and the participating spouse) were found to be in even more agreement than clergy and spouses in general, with one area of exception: the differences in perspective concerning home and family life, reported below, were generally as common among husband and wife pairs as among clergy and spouses in general.

Clergy's marriages are phenomenally healthy. This is by comparison with not only the general population but also with other professionals. For example, among Lutherans (and the statistics are not significantly different among non-Lutherans in this study):

- Only 1% reported being divorced, and less than one-fourth of 1% were separated.
- 75% and 80% of clergy and spouses respectively declare that they never contemplate divorce, and only 2%–3% say that they think of it frequently.
- 54% of clergy and 80% of their spouses say they never think of infidelity, and only 6% and 4% respectively admitted to ever having been unfaithful.
- Both pastors and their spouses overwhelmingly (63% and 79%) report that in time of trouble the first person they turn to for help is their spouse.

Common Perspectives, Especially about Ministry

Furthermore, the perspectives of pastors and spouses on various areas of ministry are remarkably similar. When asked to judge how positively their pastor spouses felt about different aspects of ministry, spouses gave essentially the same answers as pastors, except concerning counseling and administration. There clergy were more likely to say ''middling'' and spouses were more likely to say ''most positive.'' And regarding special group work, they differed in terms of clergy leaning more toward a ''less than middling'' rating than their spouses imagined, with spouses leaning more toward a rating of ''nearly'' or ''most positive'' than clergy reported.

Spouses were also unusually able to judge the levels of satisfaction that clergy would report about different aspects of ministry. Their judgments were significantly different (more critical) for only 5 of 19 ministry-related potential sources of satisfaction/dissatisfaction. However, spouses were more lenient in their judgments of what might motivate pastors' dissatisfaction with their own prayer life. (See Table 3-1.)

Table 3-1

More frequent response of clergy	Issue	Spouse's more frequent estimate of clergy's response
Very satisfied	Nurturing support received from the congregation	So-so
Very satisfied	Spouse's close identification with pastor's work	So-so to satisfied
Satisfied	Pastor's faithfulness to own sense of call	Very satisfied
Satisfied or very satisfied	Opportunity for advancement	Very dissatisfied to so-so
Very dissatisfied to so-so	Pastor's prayer life	Satisfied to very satisfied
Own lack of initiative	What might motivate pastor's dissatisfaction with own prayer life	Lack of time and energy

Clergy and spouses on the average both gave generally the same rank order to eight of nine personal activities as sources of satisfaction, beginning with the highest: time alone with my spouse, time alone with my family, friendship, time alone with myself (hobbies, etc.), physical exercise, full- or part-time studies, group recreation, and community service. The one exception was "to stimulate lay ministry"; though it was generally rated low, more clergy put it near the top, while more spouses put it last as a source of personal satisfaction.

They differed in how they rated their overall satisfaction with their self-development and fulfillment of their own personal goals, with more clergy replying that they were satisfied or very satisfied and more spouses reporting that they were unsure or both satisfied and unsatisfied.

Sometimes Disparate Perspectives on Life in the Ministry

Though they experience essentially the same amount of stress from 20 different aspects of life in the ministry, spouses on the average have a greater tendency to report somewhat serious or very serious stress—while clergy are more inclined to report no stress—from three sources: income, too great mobility, and loneliness or isolation. Both women clergy and their spouses, however, are much more inclined to report "very serious stress" over income (about 25% of both report it) and over both role expectations and conforming to them (35% of women clergy and 25% of their spouses for both). And while their spouses are about equally inclined as other spouses to report very serious stress over loneliness and isolation (about 12%), and are less inclined than other spouses to report very serious stress over privacy needs (none), women clergy report very serious stress over both in much greater proportions than do other clergy (24% and 12% for the two by women versus 6% and 4% by male clergy).

Spouses are also more likely to make certain recommendations as ways of generally improving the lives of clergy:

- higher salaries (spouses 72% versus clergy 53%)
- opportunities for continuing education for pastors and spouses (73% versus 56%)
- counseling for clergy families (65% versus 44%)
- opportunities for more contact with other clergy families (44% versus 33%)
- babysitting and childcare allowances (21% versus 12%)
- income adequate for purchase of a home (68% versus 48%)
- better sources of help in times of personal troubles (67% versus 51%).

On three of nine aspects of the spouse's potential role in the congregation about which couples were asked, spouses and clergy tend to differ in what they think or in what they believe their congregations think; while more clergy agree or are not sure, more spouses strongly disagree that the spouse should always publicly be supportive of the pastor's ministry. And more clergy disagree, while more spouses are not sure or strongly agree that:

- spouses should (and also congregations think spouses should) actively take part in decision making in the church, even when that involves disagreement with the pastor, and
- spouses should (and also congregations think spouses should) actively take part in decision making in the church, even when that involves disagreement with other lay people.

Though clergy are generally more inclined to disagree or strongly disagree, and to be little bothered that they do not have enough money to make ends meet and that they may not have enough financial security for retirement, spouses are more inclined to strongly agree and to be "quite" or "very" bothered by both.

Consistent with this, clergy are more inclined to deny any feeling of pressure to get a job, while spouses are more likely to "tend to disagree" or "tend to agree," "agree," or "strongly agree," and to be somewhat, quite, or very bothered by it. Also, spouses are more likely to agree or strongly agree that "A woman's career should be secondary to her husband's" and to be "somewhat" or "very" bothered by it.

Clergy, also, are more likely to deny having feelings of anxiety and depression. While more spouses agree or even strongly agree, more clergy tend to disagree or even strongly disagree with each of the following statements:

- "Before a difficult day, I usually find it hard to sleep because of being preoccupied with anxiety."
- After a hectic day it's usually impossible for me to keep from replaying in my mind things that happened."
- "I get into moods where I can't seem to cheer up."

About the first two of the same statements clergy are more likely to report "never bothered" or "little bothered," but spouses more frequently report "somewhat bothered" or "very bothered."

Clergy are also more likely definitely to deny that their spiritual life is in trouble, while spouses in greater numbers only "tend to disagree" or even "tend to agree."

Clergy and their spouses also characteristically differ in the degree to which they like their work. Seventy-seven percent of clergy agree or strongly agree with the statement "I like my work" (58% of spouses), yet they are more inclined to agree that their life-styles make them high risks for a heart attack than are their spouses, who are more likely strongly to disagree when describing themselves in this respect.

Sometimes Disparate Perspectives on Home and Family Life

Lutheran clergy and spouses display two different and consistent patterns of description of how they experience several important aspects of home and family life. Despite the apparent phenomenal health of clergy marriages in general, home and family life are often where the problems are when they occur.

The patterns that show potential for difficulty, if not actual problems in and of themselves, consist of more spouses than clergy definitely describing conflicts and tensions and feeling definitely "somewhat" if not "quite" or "very" bothered by them, while more clergy than spouses are disagreeing and denying that they exist, and declaring that they are "little bothered" or have "never been bothered" by them. Whether this is a difference in experience, a difference in awareness, or a difference in willingness to acknowledge or reveal a reality is not shown by the survey. But the following differences in responses to statements describing home and family life were revealed in the survey.

There are slight variations but, as a general pattern, clergy tend more to disagree or strongly disagree, and to report never being bothered or little bothered by each of the following; spouses are likely only to "tend to disagree" or rather to "tend to agree," "agree," or "strongly agree" with each of the following.

- "I am inclined to blow up—lose my temper—rather than maintain a reasoned approach."
- "I get little help from my spouse in running the household" (4% versus 34% agreeing to some extent).

- "My spouse does not spend enough time with our children" (7% versus 46% agreeing to some extent).
- "I wonder if my sexual desire is adequate" (18% versus 40% agreeing to some extent).
- "I feel unable to cope with my children."
- "I can't communicate with my spouse" (16% versus 25% agreeing to some extent).
- "I don't feel good about my appearance."

Furthermore, significantly more clergy than spouses report "no stress," while significantly more spouses report "somewhat serious" or "very serious stress" from "conflicts with spouse" and "conflict with own children."

Conversely, clergy are more apt to report being somewhat, quite, or very bothered by "My spouse is not as sexually interested in me as I would like," while spouses are more apt to say "never bothered" by that.

In addition clergy are more likely to report being never or little bothered, while spouses are more likely to report being quite or very bothered by these:

- "Husbands and wives should share responsibility for household duties."
- "A mother should have primary responsibility for the care and nurture of children."

However, spouses are also more apt to report being "never bothered" while clergy are more apt to say "little bothered" in their responses to the statement, "I am inclined to stuff my feelings rather than express them directly."

Interpretation and Reflections

The Parsonage Family

The data present an overwhelming testimony to the health of clergy marriages. The large majority of these couples tend to feel good about their marriage, are companionate, share in the work of the church, do not commit adultery and rarely even consider it, and rarely consider divorce. Compared to other professionals or even a cross section of society, these marriages stand out positively. A spouse wrote, "There seems to be a need for clergy and spouses to feel positive about themselves and to see their value to the congregation—even if that value has poor tangible rewards." These words convey the "team" concept that frequently goes with clergy marriages regarding parish ministry and how the couple's relationship to the congregation affects not only their marriage but their feelings toward themselves. From the data it appears that more often than not these feelings are good.

This apparent health of clergy marriages is a reflection of the influential role of the parsonage family in American history. The people who have come from parsonages have played significant roles in the public as well as private sectors: education, health and welfare, government, business, and the institution of the church itself. Walter Mondale and Martin Luther King Jr. are among contemporary examples. Despite the possible advantages of a celibate clergy, the Roman Catholic church has deprived itself of this potential of the parsonage family—even for the replenishing of its own clergy and religious ranks.

The good news about the state of clergy marriages may be surprising in the light of all that we hear about clergy family conflict and divorce. Bishops and other church officials are often weighed down by the numbers and severity of these family conflicts in their diocese or district. The data from the questionnaires confirm the reality of these unhappy situations. In fact, it is painful to read the hurting comments of those whose marriages are in trouble. Because of the context in which these conflicts occur—the parish community and the religiously symbolic role of the clergy—they stand out more than the marital crises of others. They also produce more pain, not only because the parish community shares in the pain but also because they disrupt the work of the clergy. Work can go on for a lawyer, a physician, a teacher, a social worker, a nurse, and even a psychiatrist if his or her marriage collapses, but when this happens to parish pastors, their work is in crisis. Some survive it by moving to another parish; some even survive within the same parish; but many have left or have been forced to leave the office of the ministry because of it, often with bruised and even negative feelings, frequently toward the church. Even though in this chapter we are documenting the health of clergy marriages, we shall attempt also to be helpful to those troubled clergy marriages that do exist.

Spouses' Accurate Perception of Clergy

The spouses of clergy tend to have an accurate perception of who their clergy spouses are and how the clergy perceive their own situation. This is another sign of an intimate marriage. Even when they differ from clergy self-perceptions, these differences are understandable. Usually, they rate the clergy higher than clergy do themselves. Even in clergy's lack of satisfaction in their devotional life, spouses tend to account for this deficiency as a problem of time pressures, while clergy themselves tend to see it as a lack of motivation. We tend to be harder than others on ourselves and, in good marriages, mates tend to be more supportive than critical.

But even in these good marriages, the clergy spouses tend to be more aware of problems in the family and in the congregation and in themselves than are the clergy. We may ask why this should be. Since the great preponderance of clergy are men and spouses are women, is it because men are more inclined to deny problems, particularly in their marriage and family, than are women? Or are women more sensitive—and thus more critical—than men? Are women more holistic in their appraisals, thereby taking in more data, while men are more analytical in their perception— more reductionist—therefore screening out more data?

Or does the difference center in the clergy profession itself? Do clergy sense a pressure to "have it all together" and, hence, have a need to screen out data threatening to this image? Is the spouse less identified with the ministerial role and, hence, more objective in seeing the problems? Or is it because typical clergy professional practice has negative consequences for the spouse in some respects, whereas it does not for the clergy? (For example, because of when lay leaders are available, clergy attend large numbers of evening meetings, and even though they may be inclined to take compensating time earlier in the day, they cannot as easily spend it with their children, who are then in school, thus leaving the spouse with more responsibility for the children.) Or is it that the spouse lacks the power and control in the congregation in spite of her status and, hence, feels more vulnerable, if not frustrated, in its problems? Perhaps all of these—and more—play their role in accounting for this difference in the awareness of difficulties. But our main concern deals with the *nature* of these spouses' concerns.

Spouses' Concerns

Again, since the great majority of spouses are women, these concerns are what one might expect. The spouses are more aware of problems with their children and with the educational and cultural deficiencies in the community in regard to their children than are the clergy. This is their mother's *role*. In this same vein, they are concerned that their clergy spouses do not spend enough time with their children and that they do not take their share of household responsibilities. These concerns are typical of our society, in which fathers experience little pressure from the culture to be "good" fathers, while mothers are under a great deal of pressure to be "good" mothers.

Yet this emphasis is changing. Equality in both child-rearing and household responsibilities is on the rise. Yet the nature of the pastor's work may slow the change in the parsonage. It is difficult to "limit the Lord's work"! This may be one of the reasons why spouses also tend to be more critical of the congregation's nurture of clergy and family than are clergy. Perhaps spouses see the congregation as demanding too much of the pastor's time and energy. Another reason may be that the spouse is naturally protective toward her clergy spouse and, therefore, may even be more critical of her husband's critics than is he.

Spouses are also concerned about their own role in life. Like other women in our culture, they feel the pressure to work outside the home. When they do take such a job, it often radically alters the family systems. Describing this change in his own situation, a clergy husband wrote, "I think the health of my parish ministry has improved since my wife began full-time employment outside the home. Our family life has also improved, for I now have to contribute more time and effort to the care of our children and to household chores. Family time has become more precious, and this has assisted me in saying 'No' or 'I'll handle that later.' The family now feels that they are more important and do not always have to take second, third, or even fourth place. I also feel less resentment towards my parish duties. I don't see the parish as the enemy of my family."

Apparently, it took this change in his wife's role in the family to bring about the changes also in his roles as husband and father and, hence, a different response from his children. Also, it provided the motivation he needed to structure in his own mind his role with the congregation. It should also be said, however, that working outside the home can create its own problems for the clergy spouse and family, mainly in the amount of time and energy that the job takes, leaving less time and energy for other needs, concerns, and interests.

Even when parsonage wives work outside their homes, they usually consider their careers as secondary to their husbands. This, too, is a cultural characteristic. Yet, it bothers many of these spouses that this is so. Again, their "bothers" reflect a change taking place in our culture. The equality of women and

women's roles in society is challenging our assumptions about
male priorities in jobs. Again, the clergy family may be slow in
reflecting this change because of the religious nature of the husband's work. The concept of the divine call is heavily weighed
in the direction of the clergy spouse. Historically, we have been
slow, if not stymied, in applying Luther's understanding of the
call to the contemporary job scene. The idea that God calls people
to all lawful occupations and not just to the office of the ministry
has remained largely an abstraction. The rise of the women's
rights movement may now force us to take seriously this Ref-
ormation doctrine of the call. Does not a spouse pursuing a career
outside her home also have a call? Clergy families are wrestling
with this question when the clergy spouse receives a call to another
congregation; heretofore, it would be assumed that only *he* had
a call. Recently, I chatted with a clergy couple in late mid-life
who are faced with this situation. She will receive her Ph.D.
degree and will be looking for a job. Since the area in which he
is pastor does not contain many opportunities for her specialty,
he has decided that this time—in contrast to four previous
moves—he will follow her. "I will look around for what I can
do wherever she gets a job," he said.

The emphasis on equal responsibility in parenthood is also
forcing us to take seriously Luther's understanding of the call.
One is called to one's *family* and *community* responsibilities as
well as to one's *job*. We have taken this seriously with the mother
role, but much less so with the father role. So fathers, even clergy
fathers, could allow the brunt of this responsibility to fall on the
mother without acknowledging their "unfaithfulness" to their
own divine call. It now appears that changes in our secular society
have forced us back to our religious roots.

Spouses are less satisfied with their work outside the home than
are clergy. One of the reasons may be that, as yet, women do
not have equal access to the more productive and creative jobs
in our society. Businesses do not always make support services

available so that women can work full time, and part-time employment is considered less significant to the company. Another may be that it is difficult to match the office of the ministry as a challenging and satisfying vocation. While some, of course, chafe under the demands and expectations of this task—and often with good reason—according to the data, a large majority of parish clergy find their work satisfying and fulfilling.

Spouses also are more likely to say that their spiritual life is in trouble than are clergy. Again, the difference may be in the pressure on clergy to be models of ''spirituality.'' Or, are women more sensitive to a diversity of data and, therefore, tend to be more critical in their evaluation of something as holistic in its comprehensiveness as spirituality?

Another difference between spouses and clergy is in their sexual desires. While there are exceptions and even reversals, the trend is that female spouses were more likely than male clergy to wonder if their sexual desire was adequate, while male clergy were more likely to be bothered than their spouses by their spouse not being as sexually interested in them as they would like. Is this difference simply a typical reflection of sexual differences among marital partners in our culture? Even so, this typical reflection is changing. Women's liberation is liberation also from sexual submissiveness. Being free to be sexually initiating, as well as being free from guilt in saying no, supposedly liberates sexual desire. Perhaps the sexual revolution has been slow to catch up with parsonage families—or perhaps it doesn't change things as much as some had thought.

A more likely reason for the difference is that it is related to the other concerns of parsonage spouses. Being holistic in their sensitivity, women are sexually stimulated by their good feelings toward their spouse and themselves. If they are inwardly resentful that their husbands do not share their parenthood and household responsibilities, if they are not satisfied in their jobs outside the home, and for these and other reasons do not feel good about themselves, their sexual desire may be diminished. Since they are more likely also to be aware of deficiencies in their communication with their spouses than are their clergy spouses, this deficiency can reflect itself in their sexual communication. Also, since spouses tend more than clergy not to feel good about their appearance, such misgivings could lower their self-image and thus dampen how they feel about themselves and their sexuality. This, of course, is particularly likely in our society, in which attractiveness is so important to a woman's identity.

On the other hand, the male spouse may seek a pleasant distraction in sex when other matters in his life are less than satisfying. Of course, there are men and women who show the reverse of these trends. As a counselor, however, I would seek to remove these obstacles to their feeling good about themselves and their spouse, as a way of reviving their sexual desire.

An Overdependent Relationship?

As we have seen, the spouse is the one to whom clergy are most likely to turn for counsel and also the one with whom to spend time provides the greatest satisfaction. In the light of this attraction, one wonders why couple devotions are not more satisfying. Perhaps this is because in couple devotions a different system comes into being than in other companionate pursuits. The relationship of each with God, as well as with each other, comes to the fore in couple devotions, which makes such devotions more than a couple relationship. When spouses are praying together, each becomes conscious of the presence of God and his or her relationship with God, which may not be the case when they make love or play tennis together. The occupational nature of praying with others might have its inhibiting influence when one seeks to be apart from the occupation. Here again, it may be the difficulty of being religious when in a religious vocation.

Though clergy and spouses tend to be highly companionable, there is the possibility that this relationship may be overly exclusive. The same data show that if a pastor is close to his spouse, he may be lacking other intimate friends. Since most clergy are men, this may again be a reflection of men in our culture. Because of their need to convey a self-reliant image, men tend not to have the intimate relationships with other men that women seem to have with other women. Men do many things together, particularly in sports, but they are not inclined to reveal their inner life, particularly their vulnerable feelings, to each other. While it appears as a positive factor that clergy share their problems primarily with their spouses, it is difficult for the spouse to be sufficiently detached when these problems concern the congregation. This puts a strain on the spouse's relationships within the congregation in her identification with her husband. Her relationship with the persons involved tends, then, to be colored by her role as her husband's confidante. By the same token, sharing with her husband her conflicts with members of the congregation may add to *his* tension in his relationships with these people. Because of what could be seen as a triangle of clergy, spouse, and congregation, the parsonage family can easily become an example of an isolated family in the midst of a potential extended family, namely, the parish community. This is due, of course, to the peculiar relationship of the clergy family—in distinction from other families within the congregation—to the congregation, and the apparent limits in their interrelationships in comparison to those of these other families. Since this is not a healthy situation, what can be done to improve it?

Unique Situation

The parish ministry is a unique situation for a family in that an organized community comes with the job. In this organized community, the clergy, spouse, and children all have a ready-made place in the community as they enter it. This provides the family with an initial security in the new community, a sense of being cared for, a place of status, and even a sense of importance.

It is also unique in that the whole family is related to the ministry—to the ''job''—and all can feel its *divine* importance. These advantages are hard to duplicate and probably account, to some extent, for the positive condition of so many parsonage families. We clergy who have left the parish for specialized ministries often comment together on what we have missed as families in these moves. In specialized ministries, there is rarely a community that includes even the clergy, let alone the spouse and children, so the family as well as the couple have to work at establishing a place for themselves in the community. For those not accustomed to this challenge, the first year or two can be a difficult social adjustment. The president of the church college to which I had accepted a call following my parish ministry informed me that he dreaded those first years with new teachers and their families who had come from the parish ministry because they had a difficult time making the adjustment. We found we were no exception to this pattern.

There are also disadvantages in this unique situation of having a place in a ready-made community, and these may contribute to the unhappiness of a minority of clergy families. These disadvantages are implied in the data and made explicit in the comments. They are also made explicit in all of the clergy/spouse workshops and other gatherings in which I have been involved. What I have done in these situations is to have the group divide into small units and share with each other where they see the need for assistance in parsonage living. There is a certain unanimity that surfaces as they share these awarenesses with the entire group. The need for assistance—which highlights the disadvantages in parsonage living—tends to focus in three areas: preserving one's privacy, preserving one's freedom, and, amazingly, overcoming one's loneliness. We shall discuss these in that order.

1. Preserving one's privacy

One threat to this privacy is the pressure parsonage people may feel to live up to the stereotypes of a pastor, a pastor's spouse, or pastor's children. I know of one parsonage family who were determined these stereotypes would not affect their children. They talked things over with the congregation, and all seemed to understand. One day, however, one of the children, along with others, got into some trouble at school. In reprimanding the students, the principal (who was not a member of the congregation) said to their child, "The others I can understand, but you, a minister's child, I don't understand." The mother was furious when she heard about this. "When it's not the congregation," she said, "it's the public school. How do you get away from these pressures?" Needless to say, she had a talk with the principal.

In our clergy/spouse workshops, the couples put on skits illustrating problems in parsonage living. In these, the telephone is consistently presented as the number one threat to privacy. Usually, these telephone interruptions are made possible also by clergy guilt. If one wants to convey the image of the always available pastor, it is difficult to evade the tyranny of the phone other than by leaving town. For a time, we had a family living with us in the parsonage who were members of the congregation, and they would answer the phone when we were not home. On one occasion in giving me the message, one of the family said, "Pastor, these people want to know where you folks are when you aren't here." For some reason, we were able to take this with a sense of humor and, in that spirit, merely responded with, "Do they?" and let it go at that.

The way to preserve privacy in parsonage living is for the family to create its own privacy. To do this, both clergy and spouse have first to deal with their guilt. Is this guilt over not being always available or not always living up to everybody's expectations a guilt before God—which is the Christian way of relating guilt to sin—or is it guilt before the internalized mores of our social environment and our image of its expectation of us? The latter is a description of Freud's superego and differs from a theological understanding of conscience, in which conscience is placed under the Word of God. Evaluating our guilt, rather than automatically trying to appease it, is a Christian obligation. It amounts to clarifying our thinking about whom we worship.

In separating our guilt before God from our superego guilt, we will have a clearer picture of where the boundaries lie between obligations to the congregation and obligations to ourselves and to our family. One can be serving God in all three. Once we see the boundaries—and these, of course, need to be amenable to the exigencies of daily living—we need then to affirm them—sensitively, kindly, and firmly. Both the congregation and the parsonage family depend on the clergy and clergy spouse knowing where these boundaries are and holding to them. Take the matter of the telephone, for example. Many times when dining in a parish pastor's home I have been disturbed to see that pastor called to the phone and abandoning those at the table for five, even ten minutes. In this situation whoever answers the phone could inform the caller that the pastor is eating and ask whether it is feasible for the pastor to return the call.

2. Preservation of freedom

The impingement on freedom in parsonage living is closely related to the invasion of privacy. Once again, the obligation is on the clergy family to use their freedom to decide which freedoms they will give up and which they will not. There is nothing unusual about clergy families in this regard, compared to the families of other professionals or business people, except that the congregation will probably be more flexible than the company. While the excellent companies, for example, described in *In Search of Excellence*, give much to their employees, they also can demand much, both in time and energy.[1] Employees who decide to limit those demands risk the company's displeasure, which, in turn, might decide that such employees do not fit into their "family," or at least do not qualify for promotion. So, in making decisions along with the congregation about how they will preserve their freedom, the clergy and clergy spouses are also modeling for others. The pastor can be more helpful to other parents caught in this bind between job and family, as he or she has worked through this bind to a livable resolution.

The congregation does not have the power—and probably does not want it—to take away our freedom, unless we give it that power. This statement may seem harsh, unfeeling, and even ridiculous when you feel helpless before these pressures, yet it remains a reality we all must face. We lose our freedom because we are vulnerable to losing it. In a sense, we are coconspirators, albeit subconsciously, in this loss. So long as we present ourselves, even to ourselves, as victims, as helpless, nothing will change. It is only when we accept our responsibility for whatever part we play in these bondages that freedom becomes a possibility. This also means giving up the secondary gains that come from believing that we are helpless, including absolving ourselves from responsibility.

A particular facet of this infringement on freedom is the pressure the clergy family feels to have a model marriage and a model family. We clergy cannot get around the fact that we are models—nor do I believe we should, even if we want to. Rather, our freedom in this matter consists in deciding what we will model and how we will model. We can model being genuine and honest people, open and caring. We can model what it means to be free to grow rather than to provide evidence that we have arrived. Succumbing to the assumed pressure to model "having it all together" leads to the denial of our problems, the erection of facades, the Sunday smiles that go with the Sunday clothes, the loss of basic leveling, and the denial of our basic needs.

Once when praying before a meal the prayer, "Bless this food, O Lord, to our use and us to thy service, and keep us ever mindful of the needs of others," a guest continued on by praying, "and keep us mindful of our own needs as well." She was "right on!" It is necessary to take our own needs seriously, not only for our own sakes but also for the sake of our family and congregation. Otherwise, we will indirectly and even subconsciously attempt to meet these needs in what is ostensibly a ministry of caring for others. One may, for example, subconsciously prolong a counseling relationship in which one is receiving satisfactions that are not being met by one's own intimate relationships. We have not arrived, but we are on the way. We are not already perfect, but we press on (Phil. 3:12).

The clergy family's place in the congregation needs to be structured. Such structuring should be a joint procedure of clergy and congregation in which individual differences are respected. Each clergy family is unique and not to be compared with previous ones. Congregations tend to respond to structure. Most people do not want to impinge on the clergy's freedom. They need to know through sharing and consensus where the lines are drawn so that they can respect them—or even utilize opportunities of ministry that come to light for them as a result of the discussion.

There will be resentments on the clergy family's part when they do not affirm themselves—when they let things happen rather than take responsibility under God for their own lives, their own roles. A wise pastor commented in the questionnaire, "A submissive spouse, especially because of some mystique about the ministry, is subject to frustration and feelings of unfulfillment. I believe that more conferences and pastoral gatherings need to give emphasis to equal participation by husband and wife and to a recognition of partnership in their full lives together." What better modeling can be given than to be our *own* person, our *own* marriage, our *own* family.

3. Overcoming our loneliness

The loneliness that a parsonage family can experience is not due to their having no place in the congregational community, but rather to the *special* place they have, which, unfortunately, can set them apart. This "set-apartness" is not the result of congregational maliciousness but of their treating the parsonage family as they have been conditioned historically to perceive them. This means that the parsonage family will need to take the initiative in meeting their own needs for intimate friendships.

Such initiative can begin with an educational project in regard to the congregation. Many parishes need reconditioning in their relationship to the parsonage family. Such a project could consist of a frank facing of parsonage family needs and ways and means in which the congregation can assist in meeting them.

The parsonage family itself needs to realize that all of its members have a need for friendship, including clergy and spouse. As a family and/or as a couple, they can brainstorm together concerning their options for securing friendships. The congregational community contains the potential for such friendships. There are risks, however, particularly for the clergy, in this area, which we shall discuss. Yet, there are risks also in not having intimate friends. If it is a choice between clergy and spouse having friends in the congregation or not having friends, the choice is obviously to have friends in the congregation.

These risks center in the fact that the clergy and spouse "wear more than one hat" with congregational friends. Therefore, such friendships may need to be structured from the beginning so that they are not confused with having political influence in the congregation. Both clergy and spouse are more free of this complication when they cultivate friendships with people outside the congregation—neighbors, other clergy and spouses, other professional people in the community—but such friendships are not necessarily more satisfying. When the friendships are within the congregation, the parsonage family would not want others in the parish community to feel excluded by these friendships. Therefore, in any public gathering of the community, it is important for them to seek out others with whom to mingle and converse.

The Basic Liberation

Two movements in our recent history have encouraged people to seek more from their lives than they are apparently receiving. These are the human potential movement and the women's liberation movement, and both have influenced the parsonage family. Based on the realization that we develop only a small portion of our potential, the human potential movement attempts to show people they can raise that portion for their own fulfillment. The women's movement is based on the realization that women are subordinate to men in our culture and that this subordination has stifled women in the development of their own identity. Both are good movements and long overdue, but they have contributed to domestic problems when they have stimulated discontent and helped to rationalize self-centered actions. In such a state of mind, I might conclude that if my present situation is blocking my identity, my fulfillment, my growth, then no matter who gets hurt, I will have to take those steps that will emancipate me. Some of these steps have hastened the breakup of marriages and families that might otherwise have endured.

What is needed for all liberation movements is the liberation of the gospel. This is the liberation that is basic to all liberations because it is the liberation of the spirit. As the captives are liberated from their bondage to pride and from the prison of self-centeredness, they can be genuinely free to care for themselves and their neighbors as they cope with their social environment (Luke 4:18).

The liberation of the gospel centers in the freedom to distinguish law and gospel. The confusion of these two biblical emphases stymies our personal growth and is destructive to our social relationships. In this contrast of law and gospel, the law is that which accuses us. (There are, of course, other uses and understandings of the law.) When we sense that accusation—when the Word that is heard is judgment—the law's association with the gospel moves us to confess, to repent, and to receive forgiveness so that we will be at peace with ourselves and, therefore, can extend that same peace to others.

There is no need to carry our guilt within us as a punishing weight; in fact, it is not Christian to do so. Rather, we are to receive the forgiveness that God has given us and to trust that the cross of Christ is sufficient for our forgiveness. We do not have to use our guilt as a way of punishing ourselves; in fact, we are called away from this practice.

When the Word that accuses leads us to the gospel that forgives, that same Word becomes for us the Word of promise— of vision, of inspiration, of calling. As forgiven people, free from judgment, we can ask our forgiving God to help us overcome our destructive ways—to change us. We can believe that God will do this, that God will reveal to us what we need to know about ourselves to effect change and will give us the motivation we need to act on this knowledge.

We can learn much from our guilt after we let it bring us to repentance. Because guilt is a judgment, we can use it as feedback—needed data—for insight into ourselves. After guilt has fulfilled this purpose, we need to let it go. To hold on to it would change its constructive purpose to a destructive influence.

The liberation of the Spirit through the creative tension between law and gospel gives us the sensitivity as well as firmness that we need to preserve our needed privacy. It gives us the freedom with which to protect our freedom so that we retain our identity. It provides us with the necessary humility to make the overtures for friendships—as our pride loses its imprisoning hold on us. "For freedom Christ has set us free" (Gal. 5:1).

For Your Doing

Individual

1. Turn to the questionnaire in Appendix A and answer the questions on "Detailed Concerns," part H, and "Pastor's Spouse in the Congregation," part I. Reflect on your profile.

2. Write your own description of parsonage life:

        Disadvantages   *Advantages*

a. _____   _____

b. _____   _____

c. _____   _____

d. _____   _____

e. _____   _____

f. _____   _____

g. _____   _____

Any surprises for you?

3. Relationships are made up of connections and boundaries. Describe your relationship with your:

a. Congregation

        Boundaries   *Connections*

_____   _____

_____   _____

_____   _____

_____   _____

_____   _____

_____   _____

_____   _____

_____   _____

_____   _____

b. Spouse

Boundaries	*Connections*

Create a way to share these findings with appropriate persons.

With Others

1. Discuss:
   a. *Masculine* means to me . . .
   b. *Feminine* means to me . . .
2. Fill out the "Distribution of Functions in Living Units" in Appendix C and share the results with your spouse. Note particularly the relationship of those items marked "exclusively" and "mutually shared."
3. Discuss this phrase: "Men have sex to feel good, but women need to feel good to have sex."

Denominational Leaders

1. How can you be supportive of the clergy spouse's "call to ministry" in the secular setting? Does this call for any change in judicatory call policy?

2. Sponsor a conference on the call—pastoral, family, and other—and discuss the balancing of the various calls for the satisfaction and effectiveness of roster persons and the church.
3. With the presence of women clergy, we now have maternity
   leave policies being written. Are you also supportive of pa-
   ternity leave for the sake of fathers and children? Why?

4

Learning to Live with Limits

Data Summary

A significant proportion of clergy (44%) *agree* to some extent that their life-style makes them a high risk for a heart attack. Four percent "strongly agree," 13% "agree," 27% "tend to agree." These proportions are essentially the same for all Lutheran church bodies represented in the survey; for all types of calls; for urban, suburban, and rural locations; and for the United States, Canada, and Australia. The proportion of agreement among spouses (about themselves) is significantly less (32%). The proportion of agreement is much greater (62%), and of *strong* agreement is very much greater (33%), among those dissatisfied with their devotional and prayer life. There was no difference in the proportions of clergy agreeing among those that could be characterized as personally "hurting" versus "not hurting."

How do clergy feel about their life-styles? Among clergy as a whole, there is a considerable proportion (17%) who are at least "quite" *concerned* that their life-style makes them a high risk for a heart attack (4% "very," 13% "quite," and 34% "somewhat," 33% "little," 3% "no longer," and 12% "never"). The proportions at least "quite" concerned were considerably less for spouses, but considerably more for the spiritually dissatisfied; otherwise there were no significant differences in degree of this concern among any of the subgroups mentioned above. (More detailed information about those concerned about life-style leading to heart attack is in Appendix B.)

Despite these concerns, there was a general tendency among clergy to feel good about their faithfulness to their sense of calling and about their personal satisfaction in ministry (57% and 58% respectively feeling satisfied to very satisfied).

Nevertheless, *two extreme groups* can be identified in terms of their testimonies on the positive versus the negative side of the creative opportunities and emotional rewards that go with the office of the ministry: those who are *hurting badly*, and those who are *feeling great*. They present two strikingly different profiles.

Where are they to be found? The two groups do not differ by type of call, urban/suburban/rural location, U.S./ Canadian/Australian location, or Lutheran or non-Lutheran church body. But the proportions of both of these extreme groups are much greater in the ALC than in the other Lutheran church bodies. In other words, in the ALC there are relatively more of *both* those who are "hurting badly" and those who are "feeling great"—at least as evidenced by their comments at the end of the questionnaire about the present health/unhealth of the parish ministry, and suggestions for improving it.

What are the two groups like? In terms of eight highly reliable scales, both groups on the average were equally convinced of their personal competence in the more responsive aspects of ministry and were equally sensitive to a conflict in values between society and the church. But the hurting are experiencing greater family stress and general role stress, greater sense of spiritual inadequacy, greater sense of personal competence in the less predictable and less controllable aspects of ministry, and less general confidence and satisfaction.

More specifically, the characteristic responses of the two groups to a large number of issues and questions were very different, as shown in Table 4-1.

Table 4-1

More frequent response of those *hurting badly*	Issue	More frequent response of those *feeling great*
Dissatisfied to very dissatisfied	Sense of personal accomplishment	Very satisfied
Dissatisfied to very dissatisfied	Opportunity for balanced living including time for self	Very satisfied
So-so to dissatisfied	Nurturing support from the congregation	Very satisfied
So-so to dissatisfied	Freedom to carry out ministry as one sees it	Very satisfied
So-so to dissatisfied	Recognition from officers of congregation and district	Very satisfied
So-so to dissatisfied	General satisfaction with one's ministry	Very satisfied
So-so to dissatisfied	One's achievements and fulfillment of goals	Very satisfied
So-so to dissatisfied	Relationship with the congregation	Very satisfied
So-so	Sense of doing something of value	Very satisfied
So-so	Use of one's talents	Very satisfied
So-so	Competence in one's work	Very satisfied
Somewhat to very serious stress	Time pressures	No stress
Somewhat to very serious stress	Housing	No stress
Somewhat to very serious stress	Conflict with congregation	No stress
Somewhat to very serious stress	Conflict with one's spouse	No stress

More frequent response of those *hurting badly*	Issue	More frequent response of those *feeling great*
Somewhat to very serious stress	Role expectations of self and others	No stress
Somewhat to very serious stress	Frustration over conforming to role expectations	No stress
Somewhat to very serious stress	Spiritual, devotional life	No stress
Somewhat to very serious stress	Frustration in carrying out ministry as one sees it	No stress
Frequent	Thoughts of suicide	Never
Frequent	Thoughts of giving one's spouse the "silent treatment"	Never
Frequent	Thoughts of resigning from the ministry	Never
Occasionally	Actually resigning from the ministry	Never
Tend to agree or agree and Somewhat, quite, or very much bothered	"I have self-doubts about my competency in ministry."	Disagree or strongly disagree and No longer or little bothered
Agree or strongly agree and Somewhat, quite, or very much bothered	"I get into moods where I can't seem to cheer up."	Disagree or strongly disagree and Never, no longer, or little bothered
Agree or strongly agree and Quite or very much bothered	"I feel angry, frustrated, or tense far too much of the time."	Disagree or strongly disagree and Never, no longer, or little bothered

More frequent response of those *hurting badly*	Issue	More frequent response of those *feeling great*
Tend to agree, agree, or strongly agree and Quite or very much bothered	"My feelings are easily hurt."	Tend to disagree, disagree, or strongly disagree and Never, no longer, or little bothered
Tend to agree, agree, or strongly agree and Quite or very much bothered	"I often feel that everything I do is an effort."	Disagree or strongly disagree and Never, no longer, or little bothered
Tend to disagree, tend to agree, or agree and Somewhat, quite, or very much bothered	"My spiritual life is in trouble."	Disagree or strongly disagree and Never, no longer, or little bothered
Disagree or strongly disagree and Quite or very much bothered	"Most of the time, I am free of tension and frustration."	Agree or strongly agree and Never, no longer, or little bothered
Disagree or strongly disagree and Somewhat, quite, or very much bothered	"I find life exciting and full of fun."	Tend to agree and Never, no longer, or little bothered
Agree or strongly agree and Quite or very much bothered	"I wish I were more efficient in my work."	Strongly disagree or tend to agree and Never, no longer, or little bothered
Tend to agree or tend to disagree and Somewhat, quite, or very much bothered	"I like my work."	Agree or strongly agree and No longer or little bothered

More frequent response of those *hurting badly*	Issue	More frequent response of those *feeling great*
Agree or strongly agree and Quite or very much bothered	"It seems that societal values rather than those of the gospel influence the way congregations and pastors evaluate success or failure."	Tend to disagree and Never, no longer, or little bothered
Tend to agree	"I find it difficult to speak on social issues because of possible controversy."	Strongly disagree

In terms of the degree to which they are or have been bothered by various negative qualities and experiences, parish pastors and chaplains present quite different profiles. Of those with various types of calls parish pastors tend to be "more" or "most bothered," while chaplains tend more frequently to report that they are "no longer bothered" by the same negative qualities and experiences.

Women clergy were found to differ characteristically from male clergy in only two significant areas. In terms of the eight highly reliable scales mentioned above, both groups on the average were equally convinced of their personal competence in both the more responsive and the less predictable and controllable aspects of ministry, equally sensitive to a conflict in values between society and the church, and equally satisfied both generally as well as with their spiritual and devotional lives. But women clergy reported experiencing *somewhat greater family stress* (primarily stress from dual careers, lack of social life or friends, and privacy needs) and *much greater general role stress* (primarily stress from role expectations of self and others, frustration in conforming to expectations, and loneliness and isolation).

Interpretation and Reflections

The data reveal a significant difference in many variables dealing with personal and professional satisfaction between those pastors who wrote that they were hurting badly and those who wrote that they were "feeling great." These comments, therefore, are of distinct importance for this chapter.

The Hurting Badly and the Feeling Good

In contrasting those who were negative in their written comments with those who were positive, it is important to note that the negative were not griping but were expressing their pain. Their suffering comes through to the reader, as the quotations used as examples will illustrate. One can feel it; these people are hurting badly. By the same token, those who were positive in their comments are feeling great, yet they are not those who use religion to deny the negative, including their pain. Those who use their religion as an escape from reality are not included in this grouping. Rather, these are clergy who both face the negative and affirm the positive. They are positive *in spite of* their awareness of problems and not because they are unaware of any problems. They say yes to life and to the ministry in spite of all the reasons they could have for saying no.

Many of these positive-minded clergy were hurting badly at one time. This comes through in their comments. "There have been times," wrote one, "when I was ready to chuck it all." Another wrote, "There have been times of serious stress—some in family relationships and some in relationships with my congregations, as well as through personal failings." Many checked the category "no longer" when indicating how bothered they were by the various tensions. This would indicate they have *moved*. We will discuss this "no longer" variable later in the chapter. One positive-minded pastor actually became positive after completing the questionnaire. "Interesting discovery," he wrote at the end. "I'm far more satisfied than I had realized."

Those who are positive-minded have something to give to those who are hurting, because they "have been there." But these positive-minded clergy themselves also express needs for which they seek satisfaction. We will address these, as well as the needs of those who are hurting.

The only area in which the small number of women clergy differ significantly from their male counterparts is in having higher stress in their role as clergy and higher stress over their family situation. These differences are understandable. Women clergy in the mainline denominations are a pioneering lot. Because of their newness to the scene, there is a shortage of role models. Their minority status is enough to cause stress in itself. The predominantly male clergy may not always rise above the sexism of our culture and treat their female counterparts with equality.

Greater family stress is also understandable. Female spouses, for example, have more of this stress than their male-clergy spouses. Women-clergy families are by and large two-income families. These also have been shown to have their particular stress. The domestic responsibilities continue to fall to the woman, even if she is working outside the home. One of our recent female graduates in this situation has resigned from her parish because being a homemaker and mother of two small children and a pastor was proving too much. The woman bears the cultural pressure placed on motherhood, in contrast to fatherhood, and can easily feel that it is up to her to make the provisions for home and child care.

It should be noted, however, that some men in this situation are assuming more responsibility for household tasks and child-rearing. It is hoped that as our society continues to change in this direction or the church takes leadership in this matter, women, and in particular women clergy, will feel less of this stress because they have only an equal share of the responsibility.

The Reality of Fallenness

Perhaps the first step in coming to grips with our pains is to recognize the kind of world in which we live and the kind of people with whom we live. The positive-minded have come to a sense of peace over this issue, while the majority of those who are hurting seem not to have done so. Instead, they often express disillusionment. A young pastor wrote, "My ideals were really shattered just a year and a half out of seminary." Another who had spent time in other work before entering the ministry saw it differently. "I love working in the church more than my previous work as a salesperson," he wrote.

How does one maintain high ideals and yet not become disillusioned in the real world where these ideals are often sacrificed to more self-centered goals? The tension between the ideal and the real is one with which all of us have to come to terms. This, of course, applies to our own behavior as well. Those who are hurting, like many of us, tend to be perfectionists. They demand much of themselves as well as others and too often feel let down by both. One of the positive-minded pastors saw this issue clearly: "The problem is not the demands of God," he wrote, "but rather the unrealistic expectations that we put on ourselves or that our success-oriented society places on us."

Part of our idealism is that we expect to be rewarded for the good things that we do. Justice would indicate this, but real people are not always ideal or just. "I feel sad," wrote one such disillusioned pastor, "that little of the loyalty and tremendous help given by my wife and family is appreciated or even noticed by the congregation. Frankly, I don't know how to deal with this."

Those who are hurting indicate through the data and their own comments that their hurts in the congregation are accompanied by hurts in the family. These family pains are expressed in particularly heartwrenching terms. The following is an example: "It was terribly depressing to fill out this questionnaire and to be reminded of long-standing marital conflicts. I have a great need to share my feelings." When there is stress at home and in the congregation, the hurting pastor often has no relief from tension—no place to which to retreat—at work or at home. The problems at home as well as those in the congregation tend to diminish the pastor's confidence. The modeling aspect of ministry—"practicing what we preach"—seems undermined by these troubles. Thus, in turn, adds to the disillusionment.

It is interesting that a psychiatrist like M. Scott Peck is drawing attention today by telling about evil in the world when our theological system has always begun there.[1] As Kierkegaard put it, "There must be a revelation from God to make manifest what sin is."[2] Without this revelation, there can be no revelation of the gospel. Essentially, the revelation about sin is that it is a perversion in the human will and that it is institutionalized in human organizations. Congregations, therefore, can behave in an evil, even demoniacal way in how they treat people—including their clergy. Some have notorious reputations in this regard. A hurting pastor in this kind of parish wrote, "I am the fourth pastor in a row that has been asked to leave by this congregation—one even left the ministry. I feel the church has poor procedures in situations like mine."

The administrative arm of the church is also criticized by pastors in terms of how they have been placed and used. "I have gifts and training that are getting underused," wrote one. This is not uncommon. Of course, the surplus of clergy accounts for some of this. Yet, some of it is also due to poor planning. To overcome this, some districts have appointed a task force to assess first the clergy applicants' gifts and strengths and then to locate the congregation in which these talents can best be used. Those, for example, with special training for urban ministry are assigned to urban rather than rural or small-town congregations, and those proficient in Spanish are assigned to Spanish-speaking areas.

While we can hope for these improvements, we should not be surprised when the fallen side of congregations and of church officials and boards comes to the fore. This awareness of fallenness helps to diminish the outrage we otherwise might experience. The same is true with our own sinfulness. We fail to meet our own ideals. We blow it, goof it up, mess up, say the wrong things, fail to say the right things—the lot! I sense in reading their comments that hurting pastors can get down on themselves as much as they can get down about the situations they are in. According to the data, both those who are hurting badly and those who are feeling great experience conflicts. They go with life in this world. But those dissatisfied with their devotional life experience more stress over these conflicts than those who are satisfied with their devotional life.

The positive-minded clergy join the hurting clergy in chafing over their creatureliness. This also is a reality we find hard to accept. "I am overwhelmed by all that needs doing," is a frequent lament. It frustrates us to no end that we are limited, finite beings. We much prefer—even long—to be infinite and unlimited like God. In fact, this is the essence of our sinfulness. In a creative, open-ended, and, to some extent, unstructured task like the parish ministry, there is literally no limit to what could and even should be done. Though the task is unlimited, the pastor, as creature, is limited.

Accepting the fallenness of congregations, church officials, and ourselves, together with the limited nature of our creatureliness as well as the creatureliness of church officials, is beginning at the beginning. Accepting a fallen reality, however, is not the same as minimizing its fallenness. It remains bad, under judgment, and in need of change, but accepting provides the starting place for coping with and changing reality. We have to begin at the spot where we are, said Kierkegaard, if we are to move from the spot where we are. The spot where we are—the present moment with all of its pain—is the only place to which we can apply our faith. And it is our faith that provides us with hope in the midst of our fallenness.

Beginning Where You Are

If you are a hurting pastor and would like to have a more positive mind toward the ministry, you need to begin by beginning where you are. This is a fallen world.

In applying our faith to where we are in our hurts, we may find its first expression a lament or protest. If you are feeling disappointed, letdown, disillusioned, your initial expression in prayer may well need to be a forthright verbalization of these negative feelings to God. In a sermon, "On Talking Back to God," Wayne Oates cites Moses as a model in prayers of protest. The strenuous task of leading a stubborn people to their promised land was getting him down. All he received from them was complaints and criticism. It all seemed so unfair and unjustified. So, he let it all hang out with God, questioning his providence. "Why hast thou dealt ill with thy servant? And why have I not found favor in thy sight, that thou dost lay the burden of all this people upon me? . . . the burden is too heavy for me. If thou wilt deal thus with me, kill me at once, if I find favor in thy sight, that I may not see my wretchedness" (Num. 11:11, 14-15).

Have you felt so despairing? Have you expressed your feelings just as despairingly to God? Moses is not the only model for prayers of protest. Our Lord himself as a New Testament Job cried out his lament from the cross, "My God, my God, why hast thou forsaken me?" He was using the familiar words of another protester, the author of Psalm 22. While we have no record of his prayers, St. Paul knew what it was like to feel forsaken in his ministry. While his direct authorship of 2 Timothy is questioned, his experience of abandonment was obviously known to the writer. "Demas, in love with this present world, has deserted me. . . . Luke alone is with me" (2 Tim. 4:10-11).

Obviously, you have lots of company. Disappointments, frustrations, betrayals, and abandonments go with life in a fallen world. So, lament and protest, for you cannot go forward until you do. As Oates says, we can "talk back to God," and when we do, "our prayer becomes more down-to-earth and real."[3]

The prayer of protest puts us in a position from which we can move to an awareness that the God to whom we are protesting is still with us. The hope will arise that his providence will not be frustrated, even though we are. The familiar words of an old hymn express this awareness.

Sometimes mid scenes of deepest gloom,
Sometimes where Eden's bowers bloom,
By waters calm, o'er troubled sea,
Still 'tis God's hand that leadeth me.

LBW 501, st. 2

Like the psalmist, in our deepest gloom, we can reflect back
to the times when Eden's bowers bloomed; on troubled seas, we
can recall those times when the waters were calm. "These things
I remember as I pour out my soul: how I went with the throng,
and led them in procession to the house of God, with glad shouts
and songs of thanksgiving" (Ps. 42:4).

This balance in memories helps us to the next stage out of our
morass, which is taking hold wherever we can—no matter how
small the endeavor—to change our situation. The place to begin
is effecting change in ourselves. While we have not been given
the power by God to change others, we have been given the power
to change ourselves—to take the log out of our own eye (Matt.
7:5).

A hurting pastor wrote, "The church needs to help me." He's
right, but the paradox is that the church can best help him when
he takes responsibility for himself in his problems. It is easy in
our down moods to slip into a "victim mentality." This is why
it is necessary to protest our lot to God with all of the emotions
that go with it. This is the spot where we are. Yet it is a spot to
move from and not to get bogged down in. While in some ways
I am a victim, in other ways, I victimize myself. Here is where
I now need to take hold. What resources do I have to effect change
in my way of behaving, responding, reacting, and fantasizing that
would exert a changing influence into my lamentable situations
and relationships? What different stimuli might I put forth that
might elicit a different response from those also involved in my
situation?

You may need to bounce these questions off another person,
a wise and trusted confidant. It is amazing how many options we
actually have, how many opportunities to do things differently,

particularly when in the lamenting stage we could see none, because we were locked into a victim mentality. Of course, these so-called stages are not chronological, but fluctuate back and forth. Yet, there is a trend, a movement, within the fluctuations toward clarity of vision and responsibility for action.

One such option was expressed by a troubled pastor—but in a hopeless sort of way. After sharing his hurts and frustrations, he concluded, "Oh, to live by the grace of God!" He's right, but he presents his option as a lament, a frustrated longing. If change begins with change in us, then we must move from lamenting, to realizing our failure, to receiving a gift. Grace is gift; if one receives it, one has it. It is unmerited, so one does not have to deserve it. It is given out of the love of the giver; the love of God is its own stimulus for God's bestowal of grace. As gospel, grace centers in the gift of reconciliation, of forgiveness, of acceptance as we are.

In the case of the troubled pastor, what does grace mean? He wrote, "I become more and more overwhelmed by all that needs to be done. Together with professional pressures, there is the need for balance in family and personal life." For him to live by the grace of God would mean that he is under no law that says he has to do it all or that he has to balance his family, personal, and professional lives. In fact, before he can even move toward these goals, he needs to receive grace—the gift that he is accepted as he is, overwhelmed and unbalanced—so that he can feel good about himself for Christ's sake in the midst of his frustration. He is loved where he is and, therefore, can love himself in his mess. This is grace. We do not have to straighten out our lives so that we can feel good about ourselves; we need to feel good about ourselves so that we can straighten out our lives.

Our laments over our inability to live by the grace of God are over the wrong issue. The lament implies that we have not received the gift, and therefore, are not living by grace. Actually, the gift is there, but we resist receiving it and, therefore, are actually sabotaging our opportunity to live by grace. Are we compelled to resist? Of course not! This is the protective illusion that needs to be dispersed.

Problems, Yes—Great Life, Yes!

Will receiving the gift calm the troubled waters and cause Eden's bowers again to bloom? Not necessarily. The change again begins with us and not with our situation. Here the positive-minded pastors have much to teach us. "Problems, yes," wrote one. "Great life, yes!" This pastor knows by experience the dialectic that runs throughout the Christian faith and life. Although the context of my life may be stormy, I can know peace in my inner life. The classical expression of this dialectic is *simul iustus et peccator*—justified and still a sinner. In the midst of negatives, we can affirm the positive, in the face of many noes, we can still say yes; in the crunch of nagging doubts, we can yet believe; in the discouragement over our own failings, we can still rejoice in our forgiveness. Problems, yes—great life, yes!

In the midst of your challenges in your ministry, you really have nothing to prove. Here again the dialectic applies. Our goals should be inspirations for our action, not measurements for our self-judgment. They are gospel-oriented and not law-oriented. One pastor put it in precisely these terms, "I feel much better since I stopped 'grading' myself so much. I will do what I can, and God will just have to do what he wants with it."

Grading has its place in our society, but it also has its limits—and beyond these it becomes counterproductive. For the past 12 years, our seminary has dispensed with the traditional grading symbols. Failure (F) is still failure, and the marginal (M) is a warning, but passing (P) is without comparative gradations. I personally was opposed to the change. I had taught previously in a college and believed grades were necessary both for evaluation and incentive. I still believe this is true for college; I no longer believe it is true for seminary. Our students have already been disciplined to study. Their motive now is to prepare for a vocation. I have been compelled by these years of evidence to realize that this motive can be stronger than that which came from the grading process. Our atmosphere for learning has improved, since one is more free to explore. Just as important, the student community is no longer concerned about a hierarchy of academic status but rather with a corporate concern, even excitement, for learning. I believe we are helping our students in this regard to move into a noncomparative, noncompetitive, supportive, and sharing esprit de corps, which may continue into the parish setting and local clergy conferences.

Even as our identity goes beyond our grades, so also it goes beyond our problems. You are not identified with either. This is good news. You have an identity apart from what you accomplish or do not accomplish. What is particularly good about this good news is that it applies *now*. You are loved *now*—unconditionally—apart from your problems, failures, successes. Your worth is a gift and is given now—apart from your reaching or not reaching your goals.

Planned Neglect

All of us, whether hurting or feeling great, need to learn to accept our limits. This comes through repeatedly in the comments of both groups. Since accepting our limits is really accepting who we are as children of God, we can see in this challenge God's call to us. Learning, in this context, means growing—growing into our identity in Christ. The category in which most of the comments focus regarding frustration with limits is that of time pressures. There is just not enough time to get it all done. Even though we all have been given the same amount of time—24 hours in a day—there seems not enough time to get it all done. We need 25-hour days and 8-day weeks, and even then we would probably still be in the same bind. Therefore, it is not more time that we need but a different attitude toward time, one that would enable us to deal with it realistically. In a sense, time is like money: we have just so much of it, now how are we going to budget it? Then we need to develop the discipline to concentrate on what we are doing in our allotments so that we become more efficient in our use of time.

So we have to work from the other end, reducing the demands to which we need to respond. One commenter called this reducing process "planned neglect." "My greatest area of frustration relates to time pressures," he wrote. "I am constantly (daily) weighing and evaluating priorities. This, of course, means 'planned neglect' of some desirable but less important things." The frustration comes from not being able to do it all; the reduction in frustration will come from accepting this reality. "Planned neglect" is a good exercise for achieving this acceptance.

The hurting pastors express this frustration with obvious agony. "What I am experiencing now in terms of stress is definitely life-threatening." This commenter sounds frightened. He is expressing a fear that many clergy—those hurting and those feeling great—entertain regarding their life-style: they "tend to agree" that their way of living makes them a high risk for a heart attack. We are threatening our ability to function and even our life span by our incessant need to be unlimited.

This counterproductive resistance to limits may begin for clergy already in their seminary training, if not before. The atmosphere in the seminaries tends to cultivate workaholism. The fact that seminary education is only a three- or four-year stint mitigates the students' concerns over the way they are living. "It will be different after we graduate"; these are the "famous last words" of seminarians. They are spoken most often to spouses who chafe under the deprivations of the seminary "grind." One of my former students rented a carrel in the seminary library in which to do his studying, even though he had a wife and four children. "I can't get any studying done in the apartment," he explained. His wife reluctantly accepted this and other neglects because "it will soon be over." But it wasn't. Like the rest of us, he was a creature of habit. In his parish ministry he found just as many demands on his time as he had in the seminary. His wife began to see the handwriting on the wall: would it ever be any different? So she ceased to be the patient and long-suffering spouse and began to complain, or in his words, "nag." During this stormy period in their relationship, he found another woman who was "more understanding."

Seminary administrators and faculties need to look upon time allotted for reflection, for private prayer, for balance in living, for relationships, for fun, as *good*. They need to model this balance in their living and teach it in their classrooms and structure the curriculum accordingly. In this way, seminaries can initiate good health habits—spiritual, mental, social, physical—to which students can become habituated while in seminary and thus take with them into the parish ministry and into their middle and older years.

Seminary needs to be a place—a community—where limits are accepted on the basis of Christian doctrine and where reality is viewed within the perspective of faith. While we as the creatures of God are limited, we believe in a creator God who is not bound by our limits. Our ministry is a joint enterprise with God. Consequently, the pastor was on target who said, "I will do what I can, and God will just have to do what he wants with it." Our boundaries point to God. Where we are limited, God continues on. St. Paul even believed this in regard to our limits in praying. "Likewise, the Spirit helps us in our weakness [limits], for we do not know how to pray as we ought, but the Spirit himself intercedes for us with sighs too deep for word [limits]" (Rom. 8:26).

We cannot do it all; with planned neglect, we can get our priorities straight. Then we can devote our efforts in a different direction—maintaining a balance in our way of living. Our ministry will be more effective when our own needs—needs based on our identity as God's children—are met. Our relationships with family and friends need cultivating for our emotional health. Our minds need stimulation from theology and from other areas of interest in God's world. Our bodies need disciplined exercise, not only for their well-being but for our total-person health. Our spirits need attention also, even though we are "up to our ears" in spiritual pursuits. Here is where the satisfying devotional life that we discussed in Chapter 2 has its need. Our devotional life is an integral part of this balance in living. Actually, it is a ministry of presence to ourselves. Brother Lawrence called it the Practice of the Presence—the presence of God and our own person in communion.

No Longer

Among the positive-minded parish clergy, a large percentage indicated that they are "no longer" bothered by the pressures and frustrations of the ministry or their own and others' limitations. The fact that they selected the category "no longer" indicates that a change had taken place in their lives. They had moved.

Institutional chaplains as a group have appreciably more "no longer" designations than parish pastors regarding their degree of disturbance over the frequently mentioned frustrations and pressures. Since virtually all of them have come from the parish ministry, this designation indicates that they are prospering under the structured environment of their present ministry, in which their limits are defined by the institution. In this setting they have clearer boundaries regarding their responsibilities. The institution sets the limits. This clarity contrasts with the vagueness in many parish settings regarding these boundaries which, in turn, lead to unnecessary pressures of guilt. Chaplains, of course, are also frustrated by their limits in that they cannot visit all the patients as they would desire, but it was my experience as a hospital chaplain that the hospital administration was much more accepting of this fact than most congregations would be. Chaplains also are usually free to be home in the evenings, so their family life has a chance to improve. As chaplains, they are part of a larger work force with whom they share similar work hours and days. This is an unspoken support both for the justification of their time structure and for the legitimacy of what they are doing. One cannot help but wonder whether one of the reasons that many of the chaplains left the parish ministry was their inability to be in control of their lives in the less structured and more varied activities of that setting.

Congregational Reinforcement

Since the change in setting has helped former parish pastors now serving as chaplains to believe they have secured more control over their lives, congregations have a real challenge to help their clergy find this same control within their parish setting. Although they can do little when clergy do not take responsibility for themselves, they can do much as partners in these responsibilities. Congregations need to realize that in calling a pastor, they are calling a priest. Priests by the very nature of their priesthood need time for reflection, for prayer, for reading, for dialoging. Each of these pursuits is related directly to all facets of their ministry and, therefore, needs to be so recognized.

Positive-minded pastors are aware of this spiritual dimension to their calling. One wrote, ''My personal spiritual pilgrimage is vital, alive, and delightful.'' It is not difficult to imagine the effect of this ''pilgrimage'' on this pastor's preaching, teaching, counseling, and administration. Contrast this comment with a lament from a pastor bogged down in the executive director role of his ministry: ''I have really been surprised at how much of this job is just a job. Much planning and administration and meetings to go to in a larger parish! Emotional and spiritual rewards are far and few between! We set goals just like in business. Periodically we review them and measure progress. There is a need for high performance from clergy. All this has a logic that I buy into. Yet, it causes tremendous stress. I feel *in* the world and *of* the world.'' Obviously, the imbalance in his ministry has been devastating.

If the congregation, and even the clergy, accept the idea that the pastorate is a job measured in ways similar to other jobs, then they ought to go the whole way and realize that even this conception won't work well without the positive reinforcement from the congregation. This is the message of *In Search of Excellence*: employees need to "stick out," to be inspired, to be rewarded with praise as well as with salary, and to be genuinely cared for and supported, if the company, factory, industry (and parish) is to prosper.[4] Denominational officials have a challenge here also. The clergy under their supervision need their reinforcement. These officials need to find out what is going on in the ministries of their clergy and give them the emotional reward they need for the good work they are doing. All of us are much more likely to do more good work if we are recognized for whatever good we are doing. "Nothing is more powerful than positive reinforcement."[5]

This does not mean that clergy should not be confronted by their congregations and denominational officials in their shortcomings, but it does mean that they should not have a steady diet of such criticism. What Charlie Shedd wrote to his daughter about her marital relationship applies also to these clergy/congregation relationships: "You can only tell him he isn't wonderful when he isn't, if you have told him he is wonderful when he is."[6]

Along with clergy reinforcement, clergy and congregations need to be clear about what each expects of the other. The boundaries need to be drawn, assumptions need to be verbalized, and a consensus reached on all of these expectations.

But structuring the expectations may not be enough in some situations. For these, the answer is simply more staff. One commenter put it well, "It would be good to keep the size of congregations at about 500 members so that a pastor can personally know his or her people." When congregations become larger than this, they should either encourage some of their members to begin a new congregation at the growing edge of their territory or call a second pastor. A veteran home missionary, a neighboring pastor in my pastoral conference, had the motto: "When a congregation reaches 500 members, it should swarm.'' He had followed this pattern in his entire ministry and, as a result, had founded several new congregations.

In contrast to this division there are clergy who are serving as solo pastors in congregations of 1000 or even 2000 members. For such pastors the workload is impossible, even if confined to essential tasks. If churches follow either the swarming principle or the principle of adding an additional pastor when their membership goes beyond 500, they would also be contributing to the easing of the mobility problems caused by a supposed oversupply of clergy.

A reason some churches and clergy may shy away from calling another pastor is the problems they fear would occur in a team ministry. A team pastor, evidently with such problems himself, commented, ''There seems to be very little done to assist team ministers work through their relationship.'' Some congregations have utilized a lay professional in the second position for a possibly easier functioning team. Yet, there are marvelous positive examples of clergy team ministries, and the resources available to congregations in conflict can be and are available to team members in conflict.

If congregational leaders—as well as denominational officials—provide parish clergy with these needed supports, their clergy might not have to leave the parish for a specialized ministry, or wait until they get a heart attack, to reach a sense of control and satisfaction in their ministry. If, as St. Paul says, every person shall receive praise from God in the *eschaton* (1 Cor. 4:5), why should we not give this praise incarnationally to those who need it in the here and now?

Reinforcement for the Congregation

What has been said regarding clergy need for reinforcement applies also to the congregation. The hurting pastors wrote many critical comments regarding their congregations. Their attitude toward their laity is decidedly negative. It is probably justified on the basis of their experiences, yet it only exacerbates the problem. By their mutual antagonism clergy and congregations only bring out the worst in each other.

On the other hand, the positive-minded pastors are lavish in their praise of their people. Probably they also deserve it, yet one cannot but surmise that there is a mutuality here also. When the congregation is praised by the pastor for what the pastor honestly appreciates, they tend to respond more positively to the pastor's ministry.

One of the hurting pastors shared some feelings about this mutuality. "I expect more from the church—yet, they are only people." Of course! Therefore, acceptance is essential as a beginning point for change. Once we move from the law—with its comparative evaluations and narrow categories—to the gospel— with its focus on the uniqueness of each individual—our experience also changes. "People give my every day a genuine variety," wrote a pastor, who, in appreciating uniqueness, is reaping the rewards of this accepting attitude. Lay people, like clergy, tend to respond to the gospel with warmth and caring; to the law, with defensiveness and withdrawal.

The message from the data and its support in the written comments is clear. This message ought not to surprise us. It is, after all, consonant with the tradition within which we receive the Good News. What should disturb us is that in spite of this, so many of us still only give it lip service as we are moved by the prevailing cultural winds that distract us in our pilgrimage.

For Your Doing

Individual

1. The hurting person has at least three major directions to channel suffering: self-blame, blame others, or let it be and live through the hurt. Describe your hurts and identify how you have responded in the categories listed above.

2. To move *from a spot*, you need to move *at the spot*. Make a list of "moves" you need to make—intellectual, spiritual, emotional, or behavioral—to move from the spot where you are.
3. Organize your "planned neglect." Make a list of those things you *need not do* to keep yourself healthy and fit. Write these into your calendar for the next six months.

With Others

1. Share events in your life that provided significant changes during the past year. Analyze your responses to those changes and answer the following questions:
   a. Do you recognize any growth that resulted?
   b. Describe the growth or retrogression that resulted.
   c. Have others been aware of growth in you of which you were unaware?
2. Make time with your friends. Seek out friendships if they have slipped away—and do the things of youthful days. Play, sing, talk, and laugh.

For Denominational Leaders

1. Make available personal and professional counseling for clergy, lay staff, spouses, and families. Our church-staff professionals, as well as the data of this research, say that service provided by persons who do not report to your office is most useful and appreciated.
2. Model self-care as a part of your leadership role. Take care of yourself spiritually, emotionally, physically, and relationally.

5

Overcoming an Adversarial Role toward the Congregation

Data Summary

Clergy are generally not enthusiastic about their prophetic ministries. There are only two ministerial activities they rate less positively: community responsibility and youth work. On the average they locate prophetic ministry exactly halfway between "not positive" and "most positive."

Among Lutherans, the situation is only slightly different. There are four activities they rate less positively: administration (about the same), community responsibility, evangelism, and youth work. ALC pastors are slightly more satisfied, and LC–MS pastors are slightly less satisfied than average. Canadian and especially Australian pastors are considerably less satisfied than Americans with their own attempts at providing a prophetic voice (average ratings of 2.9 versus 3.3). There were no differences by urban, suburban, or rural location, or by gender. Senior pastors were slightly more satisfied with their own performances as prophets.

There is good reason for the general lack of satisfaction among clergy with their own prophetic ministries. Two-fifths report that they are inclined to put off dealing with irritation and conflict, and three-fourths are at least somewhat bothered by their own tendencies in that direction.

Two of every three find it difficult to confront people with their moral and ethical responsibilities, and again three-fourths are at least somewhat bothered by that difficulty. Half report that their feelings are easily hurt, and three-fifths are at least somewhat bothered by such. One-third find it very difficult to speak on social issues because of possible controversy, while half are at least somewhat bothered by such difficulty.

It is not that they are insensitive to contrasts between cultural values and those of the church. They are generally quite aware. Ninety-three percent at least tend to agree, and 58% definitely agree that "Society seems to value success so much more than service." (Eighty-three percent report they are at least somewhat bothered by this.) Two-thirds at least tend to agree, and one-third definitely agree that "My church body seems to value success like society does." (One-fourth are at least "quite" bothered by this, and two-thirds at least "somewhat.") Forty percent at least tend to agree that "It seems that societal values rather than those of the gospel influence the way congregations and pastors evaluate success or failure." (Nearly half are at least "quite" bothered, and over four-fifths are at least "somewhat" bothered by this.) They also experience significant conflict over the contrasts they observe: one-third report being frequently torn between conflicting values, beliefs, and desires, with more than two out of five at least somewhat bothered by that experience of inner turmoil.

An Accompanying Need to Please

This minimal satisfaction with and considerable hesitation to perform prophetic ministry, a general awareness of contrasts between societal and ecclesiastical values, and considerable inner conflict over them is often accompanied by a strong need to please other people. Slightly over half report that they are too anxious to please others, and nearly three-fifths are at least somewhat bothered by that fact. Nearly 55% report that they cannot turn people down, say no, or otherwise decline others, giving priority to their own needs, without feeling guilty. And two-thirds are at least somewhat bothered by that. Also three out of five report they are inclined *not* to express their feelings directly but rather to "stuff" them. And, again, two-thirds are at least somewhat bothered by that inclination.

As additional evidence of strong general tendency or need to please, 60% report at least "somewhat serious" stress over role expectations, and half (53%) report the same level of stress over frustrations in conforming to role expectations. Also two out of every five recommend clarification of professional standards or protection of pastors from subjective evaluations as a means of generally improving the lot of clergy.

Conflict with Congregations

Considering this quite general concern always to please other people, how much conflict with congregations and stress over it do clergy report?

- Eighty-eight percent reported they were definitely satisfied to very satisfied with their present relationship with their congregations. (Only 3% were definitely dissatisfied to very dissatisfied.)
- Nevertheless, one in four reported "somewhat serious stress" over unfair treatment by parishioners, with again 3% reporting very serious stress. And one in three reported somewhat serious stress over conflicts with their congregations, with 4% reporting very serious stress.
- Two-thirds were satisfied to very satisfied with the nurturing support they receive from their congregations, one-third feeling so-so to very dissatisfied.
- Also two-thirds (not necessarily the same persons) reported sufficient communication for them to receive adequate feedback from the congregation to evaluate their ministries.

- In terms of what might improve things for clergy in general, one-third recommended more support for clergy in disputes with congregations, and very nearly one-half recommended training Ministerial Relations Committees to work with clergy and their spouses.
- One-fourth felt only so-so to very dissatisfied with the recognition they receive from officers of the congregation and with their freedom to carry out ministry as they understand it. One-third reported somewhat serious stress due to frustration in carrying out ministry as they viewed it, with 4% reporting very serious stress over it.

What characterizes those who report conflicts with the congregation as a source of "somewhat" to "serious" stress? Both those who see themselves as at risk of heart attack and those who are hurting tend to report definite stress due to conflict with congregation, while those dissatisfied with their devotional/spiritual lives do not.

Nevertheless, the profile of those in conflict most closely resembles both the profile of those dissatisfied with their devotional/spiritual lives and the profile of those who see their life-style as precursor of a heart attack—with some significant differences.

The conflicted and those dissatisfied with their spiritual/devotional lives are most similar in terms of demographics, ratings of various aspects of ministry, and dissatisfaction with various areas of congregational life and life in general.

The conflicted and those at risk are most similar in terms of overall satisfaction, sources of stress, personal attitudes, and life situation.

The conflicted are about equally similar to both the spiritually dissatisfied and those at risk in terms of what concerns or bothers them.

Those in conflict with their congregations are unique or distinctive in the following ways:

- more likely to report that their spouses, if employed, are satisfied to very satisfied with their work.

- more likely to rate the health of contemporary parish ministry as unsatisfactory or very unsatisfactory.
- being stressed by lack of mobility, and experiencing definite stress from a larger number of sources (17) than any of the other three subgroups compared above (dissatisfied = 15, at risk = 12, hurting = 8).
- recommending more support for clergy in disputes with their congregations.
- holding the opinion that congregations believe that spouses of clergy should have an equal right with other members to be considered for election to leadership, should always publicly be supportive of the pastor's ministry, should not take a leadership role beyond that of most other lay persons, and should have a right to serve the church without special obligations or privileges.

Relationships with Other Clergy

For three-fourths of clergy, relationships with other clergy and professional co-workers are satisfying to very satisfying, with only 6% dissatisfied to very dissatisfied. And only 10% reported even somewhat serious stress over other clergy's jealousy of their talents. Yet 40% at least tended to agree that "I feel the competitive pressure with brother and sister pastors to the point that it is difficult to be open and vulnerable with them," with 15% definitely to strongly agreeing.

Interpretation and Reflections

We/They Mind-set

In addition to these data from the questionnaire, 10% of those who wrote comments concerning the state of the parish ministry were critical of their congregations. These comments reveal an implicit—and sometimes explicit—"we/they" mind-set. The *we* are the pastor, spouse, and family as over against *them*—the congregation. Spouses think in these terms as much as clergy, especially when they feel their clergy spouse is being unjustly criticized. "I find 'church-going' people unforgiving and unloving," a spouse wrote in poignant, even pleading, terms. "I find it very difficult to accept the fact that so-called Christians cannot forgive when the pastor does something they do not approve of. Why? They will not let pastors be human. Why? Help!" A pastor, describing his relationship to his church council as a power struggle, wrote, "They are the 'employer' and I am the 'employee,' and thus, they think of me more as a hired hand than a pastor."

One-quarter of the complaints about the laity focus on their being apathetic toward the mission of the church and, consequently, unwilling to accept responsibility for ministry. A typical example from a woman clergy, "Many seem to think decisions and plans are to be implemented by the pastor. Congregations need to take more responsibility for congregational operations." Another commented, "I struggle with people's complacency, indifference, and apathy in regard to the life of the church and commitment to follow Christ." Another put it more bluntly, "The congregation expects us clergy to do it for them." Another predicted dire results, "As long as congregations have the attitude that the pastor works for them, pastors will be an endangered species." This comment is matched by a spouse who wrote, "This 'if no one will, we can always get the wife to do it' mentality has to go!"

Not only do the laity depicted in these comments refuse to help in the ministry of the church, they seem unaware of the burden they are thereby placing on the clergy. "The parish ministry needs help," wrote one who believed he spoke for more than himself. "Have you heard the cries? Listen and you will hear. I hear more and more of the insensitivities of congregations." This insensitivity, as we have seen from previous comments, can also be oppressive. "Too many lay people feel it is their responsibility to keep the pastor in line," commented one who evidently spoke from experience.

Twenty percent of the total number of those who wrote comments were critical of other clergy. Their complaint was largely that clergy are not sufficiently spiritual. "Wine and cheese have often replaced prayer and devotions in church," wrote a pastor who then laid the blame on "the poor role-modeling of the clergy." One focused his criticism on clergy attitudes toward congregations. "All too often, it seems to me that pastors, and especially female spouses, have sour dispositions over against their congregations." Another summed things up by writing, "Lack of prayer and spirituality in many pastors and pastors' families weakens the proclamation of the gospel today."

Another complaint of clergy concerns their competitiveness. "I am concerned that we reward competition rather than rejoice in cooperation among clergy," wrote one. "The natural ambition of pastors tends to have its abrasiveness," wrote another. The result can be lack of trust and support. A revealing comment in this regard is the following: "I probably become more tense at pastoral conferences than anywhere else." A woman clergy expressed her criticism of male clergy: "Male clergy need to work at more cooperation with women clergy and work towards more equality."

When clergy experience an adversary role with both the congregation and fellow clergy, as is sometimes the case, they become "loners." A pastor in mid-life made precisely this observation. "I'm not sure," he wrote, "that pastors find other pastors to be sympathetic friends. I think many tend to be intimidated and threatened—and lonely." These clergy are denying themselves the nurturing interrelationships of the congregation and their colleagues.

One possible indication of this loneliness is the notation of 12 clergy in the space provided for "other," that "God" or "the Lord" is the one to whom they would turn for help in their personal problems. Some of these probably wrote this as a rebuke to the authors of the questionnaire for omitting so obvious a source. What they were unable to perceive was that in listing "friend," "spouse," "fellow pastor," "bishop," etc., we were obviously asking to whom in the human community do you turn. Who within the Body ministers to you? This listing assumes the theological understanding of the church in which the Spirit ministers through the members of the body, that Christ is incarnated in his church. In making this distinction between turning to God and turning to his people, these clergy, because of their loneliness, may be slipping into a docetic approach to their faith.

Need for Mediation

A we/they attitude on the part of clergy places the congregation in an adversarial role and leads to power struggles between these clergy and their families and the congregational leadership. Once this mind-set is in effect, each "side" feels the other's coercion and resists. The result is a loss of wisdom on the part of both. Each side becomes resistant to reconciliation, because they are too threatened by the specter of "losing," too turned off by previously ill-fated attempts at compromise, and too hurt by the process. They are unable to have any objective view of the "adversary." Instead, the perspective of each is already loaded with negativity.

There is a need in these power struggles for mediation. Like families in strife, congregations and clergy need a counselor in their conflicts to assist them in clearing out the debris from their systems of perception and communication. A mediator skilled in conflict resolution is needed to help each "side" to see the interests and concerns behind the other's position and demands. Once this step is taken, new options for action become apparent that heretofore were blocked from sight by the rigid perspective of those who had become locked into stated positions. When defensiveness is overcome, wisdom returns. When reconciliation cleans out the infection, wounds begin to heal. Each may now see a potential friend where before they saw only an adversary.

This is what can happen when a win/lose mentality is replaced by a mutual motivation to find a way of functioning with which both "sides" can feel satisfied.

Denominational offices need to provide the services of such skilled mediators to clergy and congregations in their conflicts. Many are doing precisely this. One-half of the districts of the ALC negotiate for this service. There are many educational opportunities available in the area of conflict management, and persons already gifted as reconcilers need to be available to provide this service. Among Lutherans, for example, the bishops, district presidents, and their assistants of the ALC, LCA, and LC–MS have had sessions on conflict management, utilizing the resources of the Alban Institute.

While church officials have often attempted to be mediators in these conflicts, they are not always skilled in this area. The art of peacemaking goes beyond seeking compromises, and aims instead at meeting the interests and concerns of the antagonists in a mutually satisfying way.[1]

Too many pastors fear mediation by church officials because they believe it means they will be advised to leave. One of the pastors I interviewed was in the midst of a power struggle with a certain extended family in the congregation. He knew he needed help but said regarding mediation, "Something's wrong with the church headquarters when the impression is widespread that if a church official gets involved, the pastor will be asked to leave."

While this is likely an overstatement, the fact is that pastors often feel that the church official will side with the congregation, because the easiest end to the conflict is to get the pastor another call. The challenge, however, is to assist both "sides" to work through to reconciliation and to discover ways in which they can support each other and work together. With the unique resources in the Christian faith for just such reconciling action, we ought not to settle so easily for "divorce"—either in our biological families or in our church families.

Bringing Out the Best

The new perspective that can develop in the former antagonists through mediation will help them reshape their relationships. The story of what happened in an educational institution has its application to the parish. Several students came as a group to the student counselor to complain about the ineffectiveness of a particular teacher. They believed strongly that he should be terminated. The counselor listened patiently to their complaints and then made the suggestion that a plan short of termination could be tried first. Perhaps the teacher felt the rejection of the class and was suffering from a loss in confidence. If this were so, he would function better as a teacher if he felt better about himself. The plan, therefore, was that for a month the students would compliment the teacher on any possible good point in his teaching. They would gather around him after class to ask him questions and then would express appreciation for his helpfulness. After a month, the students reported to the counselor that they no longer wanted the teacher terminated. The change in his teaching was obvious to all, and the students had a new respect for his knowledge. What they had done was restore his confidence. They had also learned to focus their attention on his strengths and thus to perceive him differently.

It is this sort of approach that often occurs in the excellent companies of our country. The goal of the company managers is to assist each employee through personal attention and appreciation to develop his or her potential to the maximum. Congregations will likely discover that this approach to their clergy will have similar results. Besides being a Christian way to relate to people, it is also in their own enlightened self-interest. Clergy who believe they are valued by their people are more likely to feel good about themselves and, in turn, will be more effective in their ministry.

The same also is true regarding the clergy's approach to their lay leaders. Even as the good managers believe that people basically want to do a good job and to feel good about themselves in their work, so the good pastor believes that these leaders really want to be competent and faithful in their obligations, but that they need encouragement to believe in themselves. So, both clergy and laity should expect the best from each other and give each other the reinforcement that helps each to fulfill this expectation.

"Expect the best from people, but don't be surprised when the worst is revealed." This is the dialectic at the heart of a Christian perspective on the human scene. It is a perspective that is both positive and realistic at the same time. People created in God's image and justified by God's grace are capable of genuine care and faithfulness, yet, as fallen creatures in need of redemption, they are capable also of doing evil and even of demonic behavior. In not being surprised when people reveal their worst, we will be able better to carry on in spite of it. On the other hand, by anticipating their best, we are helping them to live up to this anticipation. Who we become and what we accomplish is influenced by those persons with whom we are in relationship. While each of us "will have to bear his own load," the paradoxical complement is that "we bear one another's burdens" (Gal. 6:2,5).

Our relationships and our ministry have a theological base. When our approach to others is law-oriented, the message we convey is "you will need to prove yourself." On the other hand, when our approach is gospel-oriented, the message is "you are loved, valued, and believed in."

Causes of Congregational Conflict

Speed Leas, who has done much research in parish conflicts in his work with the Alban Institute, lists five types of parish conflicts: (1) conflicts due to differing expectations of *roles*—for the pastor and lay leaders; (2) conflicts due to congregational *structures* in which the divisions of authority have inherent tensions that frequently reach the straining point; (3) conflicts due to *substantive* values in which there are conflicting convictions regarding how one uses the resources of the congregation and/or the faith, how one does ministry, or even, what *is* ministry; (4) conflicts due to *interpersonal* deficiencies in which persons' needs for recognition, esteem, and importance are in their estimation not being met in the dynamics of congregational life; (5) conflicts due to *ideological* factors in which clergy and congregational leaders bring into the congregational decision making their specific political/socioeconomic values as though these were identical with the values of the gospel.[2] Each of these different types of conflict may require its own particular type of intervention and approach to resolution.

In, with, under, and beyond these causes is one which Leas omits—personality clashes. These obviously can result from conflicts over roles, structures, substantive values, and interpersonal deficiencies. In fact, unless these other conflicts are well managed, they probably will end up as personality clashes. Yet, personality clashes can also be something more. There are people who because of their background, memories, and personality traits simply repel each other before they even have a chance to offend each other. They have the "wrong chemistry" or "opposite temperaments" or "are too much alike."

Because the egos of both "sides" in any of these conflicts can get projected into the conflict, the substantive issues indigenous to the conflict can become secondary to winning or losing. It is because of this tendency that those not involved in the conflict find it easy to label these conflicts as *primarily* personality clashes. Even if they were, this would not mean, as we often imply, that the conflict has become irresolvable. With skilled mediation, even when the wrong "chemical" predisposition is involved, things can change.

Ascribing conflicts to personality clashes, however, can be used to blur the substantive issues involved in the conflict when these are uncomfortable for others to face. It is an easy way for these others, including an unskilled mediator, to keep their "neu-trality." If it is a personality clash, then I as an observer think I can be absolved from the responsibility to become involved, even though the issues now hidden in the conflict have a moral and ethical dimension. For example, in Jesus' day one could have attributed the conflict between Jesus and Pharisees—or later be-tween Paul and the Judaizers—to a personality clash. Denouncing the opposition for devouring widows' houses and for pretense in making long prayers (Luke 20:47) can hardly be considered a conciliatory gesture. If we want to stay uninvolved, the volatility of the conflict could be sufficient reason. We can permit it to distract us from the moral and ethical issues that are present.

Yet, this verbal and, at times, physical violence has often char-acterized one of the vital ministries of the church. There is a potential asperity built into the *prophetic* ministry. Christians and their called and ordained leadership are by their very identity witnesses for God in the world. Theirs is the challenge to live *in* the world without being *of* it. The prophetic ministry is the min-istry that watches over this paradox. Obviously, it is a very dif-ficult ministry. People, even God's people, can react negatively, even hostilely, to it. Not only are the prophetic issues often blunt-ed by ascribing them to personality clashes; the prophetic ministry itself is frequently *interpreted* as a personal attack and reacted to in like manner.

Prophets Are Rarely Popular

Prophets are rarely popular, as history attests. "Which of the prophets did not your fathers persecute?" asked Stephen as he was being martyred (Acts 7:52). Jesus himself was crucified be-cause of his prophetic ministry. So also has it happened to his disciples. Clergy prophets have been driven from their congre-gations, bishops from their offices, and lay prophets from their jobs—often into an actual or symbolic exile because they called a spade a spade in matters of right and wrong. They may not always have had good timing or wise approaches, but they were faithful to their responsibility to discern being *in* the world from being *of* it. When we assume our prophetic responsibilities, we risk a similar fate. Naturally, people tend to avoid this responsibility, so that anything that can divert the issue to personal rather than prophetic terms is latched onto.

Clergy usually have less vested interest in the material side of this world and its values and so perhaps can see clearer the difference between these values and those of the gospel. Also, they are "set aside" so to do. The same can be said for the poor. They also are lightly invested in the socioeconomic/political mainstream of society and, therefore, have less need to protect its interests. In fact, the poor are more likely to attack these interests. This does not mean that the poor are more virtuous than the affluent. The poor simply have less need to defend the status quo.

Not being a part of the socioeconomic jungle of this world may also be a handicap. "How," asks the politician, business person, union steward, farmer, "can the clergy know what it is really like out there?" How can they know the pressures, the dilemmas, especially the ethical ones, that those "jungle fighters" face as their security and status are directly dependent on the outcome? Granted, there is no way to know what things are really like better than to be in the thick of them. Despite this handicap of the clergy, however, their dissociation from the money-as-power-and-status syndrome is perhaps necessary for the clarity of their vision. A clergy commenter saw into the dilemma. "There may be a danger ahead," he wrote, "as we improve the financial status of clergy. The 'call' will give way to the 'job.' I like getting a decent paycheck, but I don't think I should be affluent or else I'll lose touch with the people our society is already overlooking." His last sentence is a reference to the historical task of the prophet to identify with the poor, the oppressed, the discriminated against, in opposition to their oppressors and exploiters. In one sense, all clergy are affluent compared to the poor in Latin America or Asia or Africa. Yet, within the social context within which we minister, the words *affluent* and *poor* have their own comparative reality. The more free we are from the need to protect our own "investments" in the "system" the more free we are to identify with the victims of the "system."

Acculturation is the leading seducer of the churches. The difference between our cultural values and those of the gospel is easily blurred. We tend to reflect the mores of our social environment rather than be the people of God who lighten the darkness and function as societal consciences. Prophets—clergy or lay—preachers, poets, and folksingers sound the warning against acculturating tendencies. They are the "watchmen on the walls of Jerusalem" that keep us aware of the tension between the values of the faith and those of the world in which we live. It is the potential erosion of this tension that is the basis for the prophet's characteristic call to *repentance*—to *change our mind*, our values, our behavior.

Clergy Problems over the Prophetic Ministry

As we can see from the data, clergy are not happy with their prophetic ministry. Of the ministerial activities about which they feel positive, it ranks close to the bottom. One reason for this may be the hazards of this task for which clergy appear ill-suited. According to the data, they find it difficult to confront people whose behavior is ethically questionable. On the other hand, who of us relishes this duty? Yet, if our reluctance is such that we resist doing it, we may find ourselves incapacitated as prophets.

In Israel, God raised up prophets when the duly appointed priests failed to function in this capacity. While some of the prophets were priests, the prophets and priests were often in opposition to each other. The priests tended to cooperate with the dominating powers of society, while the prophets tended to oppose them. Obviously, some of us are more suited for being prophets than others. The fact remains, however, that in the parish ministry the pastor accepts this prophetic function of ministry for the people, or they will likely be deprived of it. The same is true for other functions of ministry. We are not all equally gifted in preaching, teaching, counseling, group work, or administration, but for the sake of the people, we do the best we can. While in staff ministries in larger churches ministerial functions are frequently divided, it would not only be unfair but divisive to designate one of the clergy as the prophetic minister. Some congregations, in effect, do this, but label the office Minister to the Community.

Another hazard of the prophetic task closely associated with confrontation is the possibility of displeasing people. While clergy obviously displease some people, they tend to find it hard consciously to risk such displeasure. In a summary of data from the Myers Briggs Type Indicator, clergy in ranking their preference for the basis of choice tend to make their choice at the feeling rather than the thinking level by 79% to 21% (compared to 50% for each in a general population sample). This, of course, has some advantages. Clergy as "feeling people" are considerate of others' feelings, understanding of their needs, and predisposed toward conciliation. Yet these qualities can also be problems when one needs to be more objective, reasonable, and critical—qualities associated with the "thinking person." Thinking people, however, are slower to notice people's feelings and are thus less empathetic and are more inclined to stand firm than to seek conciliation.[3]

Because clergy tend to make their choices on the basis of feelings, they may too easily give in to conciliation when firmness is needed. The need to please overrules the need to exercise what is currently called "tough love." In so doing, however, these clergy are operating under an illusion. This need to please often precipitates the very displeasing they are attempting to avoid. Their dependency on pleasing is a vulnerability which others, particularly thinking people, find it hard not to take advantage of. In a political sense, it is a weakness that can be exploited by others.

Ironically, pleasing pastors expect a reward for their conciliatory actions, and when they don't get it—or even get the opposite—they may feel justifiably outraged. What we clergy need to realize in our penchant to please is that in this pursuit we can lose our individuality—to say nothing of our prophetic role. It becomes increasingly apparent to others that we are not leveling, and, ultimately, this is not respected. A commenter summed it up well: "My perception of the present state of the parish ministry is that more pastors need to own their own personhood and quit playing the role of keeping the congregation happy or preserving harmony at any cost."

At the same time that clergy are reluctant to function as prophets, they indicate they are well aware of the contrast between our cultural values and those of the gospel. Referring to the current state of the TV media, a pastor commented, "TV undermines the church's ministry in use of time, morals, and shaping of priorities." Another wrote, "I am concerned that we now reward competition rather than rejoice in cooperation among clergy and families. We need guidance and support for standing over against the world, not encouragement to subscribe to its ways." And another, "I get nervous about borrowing assumptions and forms from a society which is based on presuppositions which are antithetical to what the church represents."

Although they are prophetically perceptive, these and other clergy—as the data indicate—tend to be silent at the crucial moments. Although we are bothered by the church's acculturation, we accommodate ourselves to it at the expense of our prophetic self-image. Some, of course, do speak, and some also get flack from their congregations. Those, for example, who have spoken against the racism of our age have often endured hostility. So also those who have spoken to the class issue. This should not be surprising. We clergy need to face up to the cross in our ministry. It is there by virtue of our being ministers of Christ. If you need a good antidote for your compulsion to please, remind yourself of Christ's own warning, "Woe to you, when all men speak well of you, for so their fathers did to the false prophets" (Luke 6:26).

Priestly-Prophetic Balance

Just speaking out as a prophet is not enough. We are called to do so effectively to encourage repentance. Just speaking out may even create resistance to repentance, depending on how we speak out. What is needed for effectiveness is a priestly-prophetic balance. We need to care about those whose values we question, and they themselves need to sense this care. Because there is a tension in this ministry, we need to condition ourselves to live positively with conflict. All ministries require patience, but the prophetic ministry even more so. In our desire to see instant change, we, in effect, are trying to sow, water, and reap in one operation. It rarely, if ever, happens in this way. While it may seem that we have at times instantly reaped, it is more likely that others before had been sowing and watering.

In proportion to our lack of patience, we may also become self-righteous—a not infrequent occupational hazard of prophets. The most effective way of "speaking out" may simply be modeling. While some have criticized clergy for being in the forefront of human rights and peace demonstrations rather than encouraging their laity to be the church's representatives, the laity are more likely to do so when the clergy lead the way. It is not unusual for "successor" pastors in a congregation to be able to be more forthright in their speaking because of "predecessor" pastors' less verbal but still effective modeling.

As a result of my sabbatical study with this questionnaire and its results, I added a new elective to our seminary curriculum: "Dealing with Conflict in and with Congregations." People from the community who were wise veterans of church conflicts were invited at each class session to assist in the teaching. The course proved to be needed. Conflict management is amazingly absent from seminary curricula as a whole—amazing because conflict is precisely what most parish clergy sooner or later find themselves in. In listing 25 "critical incidents" typical of congregational life, such as conflict over worship format, discomfort in representing own salary needs, ministry to terminal patients, and staff friction, Roy M. Oswald of the Alban Institute contends that over 75% of the skill training required in such incidents is in the areas of general human relations and interpersonal conflict.[4]

In our seminaries we tend to provide our students with the idealism for ministry—and this is good—but we are sparse with the tools to deal with the realism. Seminary students need to develop the ability to face what is negative, particularly negative feelings, in themselves and others. Then they need to learn the art of dialoging within the dynamics of these feelings in a sensible approach to conflict.

The priestly function of ministry prepares the way for the prophetic. In pastoral counseling, largely a priestly ministry to assist people to overcome their problems through the resources of the faith, one is helped to "listen" to negative feelings. Also in the clergy's ministry to the needs of others through pastoral care, preaching, teaching, and group work, people perceive that the pastor not only understands how they feel, but that he or she also cares about them. When people have this appreciation of their clergy, they will listen to them when the clergy remind them of their responsibility for their witness as God's people in this world. The clergy's ministry of caring establishes the rapport for dialoging necessary for an effective prophetic ministry.

The prophetic ministry naturally follows the priestly ministry. An example again is in pastoral counseling. Healing and becoming responsible go together. This is why confrontation is a needed art in counseling. The pastor often needs to assist people to see what they are resisting seeing because seeing would imply the necessity for their doing something about it. However, when the confrontation is successful, a change in behavioral direction usually follows. In a broad sense confrontation leads to repentance.

At the risk of again sounding critical toward my own area of ministry, theological seminaries as a whole have not prepared their students well for the prophetic ministry. Either they ignore this ministry, or they present it in an ideological framework that may not relate well to a priestly-prophetic balance. In order to correct this situation from a pastoral care point of view, at least at the graduate level, our seminary has developed a "Ministry in Pastoral Care and Social Change Graduate Program" in which the practice of pastoral care and counseling and the ministry of social concern are put together as one ministry. Students minister under supervision at various clinics and agencies in either area with a study program that treats both as a balanced and united ministry.

There is an art to the prophetic ministry as there is to the priestly ministry, and this art centers on keeping both ministries in a creative tension. Too often the prophetic ministry is left to the pulpit, where it is least likely to be effective, primarily because it needs a dialogical medium. Also, the pulpit can be abused as a protection against such dialog. Without this opportunity for dialog, the prophetic message may be perceived as judgmental. Of course, it does contain judgment, but if it "comes off" as the judgment of the authority on erring subjects, the reaction is likely to be resistance rather than repentance. If, on the other hand, the pastor has raised these prophetic questions previously in classes or forums and has encouraged dialog and respected differing opinions, his or her use of these prophetic questions in a sermon will probably be in the same dialogical spirit.

People can actually be grateful to those who keep their eye on the boundaries of being in the world but not of it—for themselves and for their congregations. Behind their—and our—defenses, they and we likely do want to live as God's people and be faithful witnesses.

For Your Doing

Individual

1. In conflicts, we tend to take *too much* or *too little* responsibility for the problem(s). List your conflicts, and assign primary responsibility as appropriate. What insight have you gained?
2. Write a "problem statement" on one or two of your conflicts. Follow this guide: *who* is doing *what* to *whom* with what *effect*? Repeat descriptions until major issues are described. Do you see a pattern?
3. Review your descriptions of shared ministry, Question 3, at the end of Chapter 1. Personally identify additional ministry settings in which you can use the skills listed.

With Others

1. With confidants, such as spouse, friend, or trusted congregational leader, examine the problem statements written above and identify your relationship to the issues. What can you do?
2. Clergy, spouse, and congregation—a dynamic triangle that can bring stress into any or all parts of the relationship. With spouse or congregational leader, review the tension points and seek a way to remove or reduce them.

For Denominational Leaders

1. Bishops are finding that they can be more effective as a "last line of defense" rather than the "first line" when conflicts erupt. Set a policy for your judicatory that spells out the conflict response pattern of your office. Check to see what other judicatories are doing.
2. Train and utilize conflict-intervention teams as you seek to support clergy, lay professionals, and congregations.

3. Many judicatories are finding that the bishop's office is strengthened as particular responsibilities are assigned to staff persons for implementation but supervised by the bishop. Describe the function of the bishop's office and then assign specific functions to the staff and hold them accountable. You can locate other resources by checking with your churchwide offices and social service agencies.

6

Utilizing Opportunities for Friendship, Retreat, and Corporate Support

Data Summary

Both clergy and their spouses were asked to reveal how much stress they and their families experienced from each of 24 common sources. The patterns of their answers showed seven separate groups of stresses among them.

Any pastor or spouse may experience stress from one or more of these groups of sources without being particularly affected by any of the others. However, persons stressed by one thing in a group tend to be equally stressed by the rest of the things in that group. In other words, the sources of stress in each group are intercorrelated. The first group is most highly intercorrelated; the seventh set is least, but still, correlated.

Five of the sets, though independent of each other, are each correlated with stress experienced from lack of mobility, i.e., perceived inability to change location when one wants.

Two of the sets, also independent of each other and the other five, are each correlated with stress experienced from too great mobility, i.e., too frequent change of address.

The five sets correlated with *lack of mobility* are:

Type 1: From conflicts with the congregation, unfair treatment by parishioners, and frustration in carrying out ministry as one views it.

Type 2: From time pressures, privacy needs, frustration in conforming to expectations, role expectations of self and others, and spiritual/devotional life.

Type 3: From loneliness/isolation, and lack of social life or friends.

Type 6: From dual careers, other clergy's jealousy of one's talents, the spouse being regarded as a pastoral extension, lack of employment opportunities for the spouse, and conflicts with one's spouse.

Type 7: From housing and income.

Type 2 is negatively correlated with stress from lack of mobility, while the other four are positively correlated with it.

The two sets that are related to stress from *too much mobility* are both positively correlated with it:

Type 4: From poor opportunities for children, lack of cultural opportunities, and community pressure on the children.

Type 5: From conflicts with one's own children and from physical health problems.

That the sources of stress that constitute Type 1 are the most tightly correlated set, does not, however, mean that they are the most common type. Sources of stress for clergy and their families, from greatest to least, are reported in Table 6-1 (p. 131). A rating of 1 = very serious stress, 2 = somewhat serious stress, and 3 = no stress.

There were no significant differences in rank order by the three major Lutheran church bodies in North America, nor between clergy and spouses. However, American, Canadian, and Australian Lutheran clergy did report significant differences in stress

Table 6-1

Rank	Average Rating	Source
1	1.90	Time pressures
2	2.31	Role expectation of self and others
3	2.35	Income
4	2.39	Frustration in conforming to expectations
5	2.41	Spiritual/devotional life
6	2.45	Frustration in carrying out ministry as one views it
7	2.47	Lack of social life/friends
8	2.51	Loneliness/isolation
9	2.55	Privacy needs
10	2.61	Conflicts with congregation
11	2.65	Conflicts with own children
12	2.67	Conflicts with spouse
13	2.68	Spouse regarded as pastoral extension
14	2.70	Unfair treatment by parishioners
15	2.71	Housing
16	2.73	Community pressure on children
17.5	2.74	Lack of mobility
17.5	2.74	Dual careers
19.5	2.76	Lack of employment for spouse
19.5	2.76	Physical health problems
21	2.80	Lack of cultural opportunities
22	2.88	Other clergy's jealousy of talents
23.5	2.89	Poor educational opportunities for children
23.5	2.89	Too great mobility

from three sources. More Americans proportionately were very seriously stressed by lack of mobility, more Canadians somewhat stressed, and more Australians not stressed. Conversely, proportionately more Australians reported very serious stress from community pressure on their children and from their spouses being regarded as pastoral extensions, more Canadians somewhat stressed by both, and more Americans not stressed by either. Also women clergy on the average gave higher ratings (indicating greater stress) than men clergy primarily to four sources of stress: role expectations of self and others, frustration in conforming to expectations, loneliness and isolation, and dual careers.

In light of this structure of stresses, what do clergy and their spouses believe will improve the lot of clergy in general? Their top three recommendations were: (1) opportunities for continuing education for pastors and their spouses, (2) clergy-family retreats and workshops, and (3) higher salaries.

Nearly as many, and about equal numbers for each, mentioned income adequate to purchase a home, counseling of clergy families, and training congregational Ministerial Relations Committees to work with clergy and their spouses.

In a comparison by country, Australian Lutheran clergy differed most frequently in the degree to which they did *not* recommend certain courses of action popular among Canadian and/ or American Lutheran clergy:

1. More opportunities for moving (100% not recommending versus 93% of Canadians and 75% of Americans).
2. More support in disputes with congregations (82% not recommending versus 73% and 65% respectively).
3. Better support from denomination, district, or synod (80% not versus 51% and 70%).
4. Training Ministerial Relations committees (78% not recommending versus 51% and 51%).
5. Higher salaries (77% not recommending versus 56% and 54%, both recommending!).
6. More contact with other clergy couples (55% not recommending versus 60% and 32%, both recommending).

The following were the most frequent kinds of recommendations offered by the approximately 5% who wrote in suggestions, in addition to the 13 choices they were given opportunity to check:

1. Training lay leaders in churchmanship, mission, understanding of life of a pastor (9%).
2. More time off/sabbaticals (with accommodations provided) (9%).

3. Improved seminary education, including some to be required for spouses (practical, spiritual, human relations) (9%).
4. More district-synod support/contact/competence (8%).
5. Improved call procedures (8%).
6. Peer support groups for clergy, spouses, women clergy (8%).
7. Realistic expectations and clarification of them (6%).
8. Better income, housing and travel allowances, and congregational education concerning them, or national church control of them (6%).
9. Training for team ministry (5%).

Interpretation and Reflections

The data for this chapter are supplemented by a rich supply of written comments in the questionnaire. The data plus these comments are essentially a response to the stresses to which clergy and their families are exposed as described in the previous chapter. Instead of permitting these conditions to lead to a heart attack, these data describe ways of coping that provide a needed balance to what can be a one-sided life-style.

Pressures and Frustrations

Time pressures lead the list of stresses. The time factor, however, is coupled with the need to be a giver with no awareness of limits on giving. One pastor even viewed the ways of coping as possibly adding to this pressure. "Allow pastors a more normal work week rather than a continuous push on use of time even for workshops." This pastor's use of the verb "allow" indicates her belief that the problem is out of her hands.

Next are those frustrations that grow out of pressures to fulfill an expected role. "We always need to be strong for them [the laity] and meet their needs," one writes, but then offers a qualifier, "I feel we have not let them help meet our needs." We will develop this need for mutuality later. Growing out of these pressures is the desire for privacy—a time and place to be nurtured.

Lack of mobility is another frustration, but it is peculiar to American clergy. Neither the Canadians nor Australians see much of a problem here. The obvious reason is our American over-supply of clergy. I find it significant that I have not heard the old familiar prayer lately in our churches: "Lord, send forth laborers into thy harvest." Obviously, we were not prepared for the answer to this biblical petition. Getting what we asked for has become a problem. The laborers are here but feel trapped in fields that they believe they have already harvested—and others are un-employed. One of our pastors wrote that he is willing to forego his normal desire for upward mobility and will settle instead for lateral mobility: "I feel we need mobility. Lateral mobility is all we can expect. But for the health of the clergy that help needs to be there."

I realize that this need for mobility places a burden on bishops and other church administrators. Yet I hope that they view it as a positive challenge. The church is looking to its administrators for the creative imagination and even risk taking that may be necessary to utilize the abundance of clergy laborers. Clergy as well as lay people want the placement of pastors to be their administrator's priority. The ALC's home mission program en-titled "50 More [new missions] in '84" had this priority as one of its motivations. This is to be commended. But more is needed—much more. Money follows priorities. We have seen this principle at work in the millions allotted to Lutheran merger negotiations. What a privilege it is to allot similar monies to enlarging our ministries as a response in stewardship to God's gift of laborers.

The result of lack of mobility—even lateral mobility—on the one hand, is negative. As the data indicate, it frustrates those who believe they should have a change, draining their enthusiasm for their present ministry. On the other hand, some have discov-ered new challenges for their own growth of which they had not previously been aware. When the option of change is not present, some have discovered other methods of dealing with their frustrations. In an article in his church paper a parish pastor stated that in having to stay and deal with his problems which he normally would have left by accepting a new call, he learned new ways of coping—of working through his problems, particularly his conflicts within the congregation—that otherwise might have eluded him.

Before taking up the suggested solutions offered by clergy to these and other stresses, we need also to consider the problem of the myths that sustain a good deal of this stress. Essentially, these are myths about who clergy are. A clergy spouse said it well, "I believe much energy is used in maintaining the image of a 'blameless character' which the congregation seemed to need." If we deal realistically and openly with this and other myths—with ourselves, our spouse, our family, our peers, and especially our parish—we will do much to emancipate ourselves from such distorted impressions.

The solutions offered by these clergy are more than stress reducers. They are essentially means for spiritual growth. As one pastor put it, "We need encouragement to grow even when things are going well."

Retreat—Place to Go

"I need a place to which I can get away to sort things out and put things back together. A retreat setting where professional guidance is available would be ideal." The pastor who said this spoke for many. Many also included the family: "Clergy families need to be provided with a center that is inexpensive where they can go to retreat and do nothing if they so desire. Available counseling at this center to help them reflect on their situations would be helpful."

A clergy friend of ours invited our family to join his family for a vacation in the Rockies at a place provided by the institution for which he worked, the Good Samaritan Society. This society's employees can use the center—actually a few cabins—without cost for specific days for which they register. Besides the glorious scenery and other opportunities in nature, this setting in the Rockies was provided with all the accoutrements of housekeeping for one, two, or three families. This opportunity seems to fulfill the picture of what these clergy who need to get away have in mind.

The word *sabbatical* was frequently used to describe this need. As a teacher, I know the value of sabbaticals. If it is beneficial for theological professors to have sabbaticals, so also parish clergy. Those few places of which I am aware where sabbaticals are being made available to parish clergy are cause for optimism. We all need a change of pace—a balance to our living—a place to go where we can without guilt get away from the phone and other obligations. Efforts in this direction by congregational leaders and district and denominational officials will be richly rewarded by growing numbers of clergy with a renewed vision and restored energy. There are several models among church districts of sabbatical programs for the pastor. One of these is described in detail later in this chapter.

A disconcerting discovery among those districts that have these programs is the lack of response to the opportunity on the part of the clergy. As one who has been on several sabbaticals, I do not consider this a mystery. Sabbaticals require planning, and because of their lack of urgency, such planning is easily postponed. Also, sabbaticals can be frightening. If one is habituated to a pattern of reacting to the pressures of the parish, one might be reluctant to expose oneself to a life-style without these pressures. Other pressures less familiar and perhaps even less manageable may take their place.

Workshops

Many commenters suggested retreats with other clergy and spouses or lay persons in which needed support could be structured under qualified leadership. Workshops are good examples of this solution. They can be structured for general purposes, such as spiritual growth, marital enrichment, or for more specific ends, such as improving communication skills or developing inner serenity.

I have taken part in, as well as conducted, many such workshops in the past decade and value this ministry highly. I can understand the clergy spouse who wrote, "Thank God for workshops!" They help people to experience the communion of saints in an existential and meaningful way. In a religious setting the workshop format consists of segments focusing on (1) Bible studies pertinent to the subject matter; (2) structured exercises in which the participants share with and listen to each other in mutual ministry; and (3) periods for group prayer and meditation.

Continuing Support Groups

Workshops and retreats provide opportunities for getting away from the work setting for a change of pace and scenery. Another solution put forth by the questionnaire respondents can take place within the work setting—support groups that meet on a regular basis. One commenter tied the two together, "Clergy/spouse retreats where concerns can be expressed need to be accompanied by suitable plans for follow-up, such as a growth group with a qualified and sensitive leader." Some support groups are confined to clergy while others include spouses, and some include also other professionals.

Support groups are a current structural expression of what have always been recognized as significant friendships. The fact that we need to organize these groups is a reflection of the kind of society in which we live. Under our cultural pressure to compete and succeed, friendships are discouraged rather than encouraged. An alternate force is needed to stem this tide, and organized support groups are one such example.

Besides the intimate family relationships of spouse and parent, the Bible also utilizes the relationship of friendship to describe the divine-human relationship. God and Jesus are both described as our "friends" (John 15:14-15; James 2:23). Because we are created in God's image, friendships, along with family ties, are needed relationships of intimacy for us humans.

While clergy meet frequently as peers in local conferences and ministeria, many of these groupings are not structured for mutual support. Too often they include the competitive spirit of our culture so that being guarded rather than open is the safest route with one's colleagues. A professional lay worker, seeing the pastor with whom she ministers deteriorating emotionally in what appeared to be a mid-life crisis, lamented his lack of peer support. "What bothers me," she said, "is the lack of camaraderie within his own denominational peer group. He has not developed any in-depth relationship with any of these clergy. They meet sometimes twice a month, and he comes away feeling lonely. My heart goes out to these ministers who can continually minister within the 'flock setting' but have never risked or taken the time or interest to minister to each other."

One day I encountered a former student in a bus depot. He had become a bus driver. He had left the parish ministry, he said, and was finding satisfaction in his present job. "What I missed in the ministry, I have here," he said. "My brothers and sisters in the union are far more of a support system than I ever had in my denominational pastors' group—and I need this support."

But some pastors do have it. One group in my community has been meeting weekly for years—even amid changing pastorates—at 6:00 A.M. for a leisurely breakfast in the back room of a local cafe. One of our commenters writes, "I believe that local pastors from clusters of congregations can form effective systems, especially when using the vehicle of weekly exegetical lectionary studies. Our own group is interdenominational and does this quite successfully."

In initiating such a group, I believe it is wise to select a person as leader who has strong group leadership skills. Such a leader will help to keep the direction clear and make sure that support is given to those who share. Local CPE supervisors may be helpful in this regard, also those with special training among the parish clergy or even a qualified person from another profession. After the group develops its own history of interreaction, a leader may not be so important. The keys to the success of the group are regularity of and commitment to the meetings and a willingness of the participants to share the intimate aspects of their lives, including their weaknesses.

Some of the commenters suggest a support group within the congregation. While at first glance the people of the congregation may be the last ones with whom the pastor would want to share his or her inner self, congregational support groups for the pastor are growing. We have several in churches in our area, including some with clergy teams. One of the things such a group does is puncture the myth that the pastor must be the strong one for the people. Here the people can be strong also for the pastor. "The support that comes through a prayer/support group has been a healing and strengthening ministry in our parish," writes a convinced pastor.

In starting such an intracongregational group, it is important that the planning for the group stresses the support nature, rather than program nature, of the group. The people chosen should be caring and open people with whom the pastor or pastors would feel comfortable in baring their soul. This does not mean that they be those who favor the programs of the pastor or are already especially close to the pastor. Rather, an attempt should be made to concentrate on the qualities of the person and to make selections from a broad spectrum of the congregation. It would be most helpful to secure a qualified leader—other than the pastor. The value of such a support group is that it helps to keep a balance for the pastor in giving and receiving within the congregation. Models are the ALC's Church Staff Support Program and the LCA's Mutual Ministry Committees.

More important than the type of support group clergy have is *that* they have one. One of our commenters provides a good conclusion: "I believe the parish ministry is challenging and exciting. More than ever, we need to encourage and develop local support groups for clergy and spouses."

Continuing Education Opportunities

The popularity for continuing education opportunities for pastors is attested by the growing number of continuing theological educational centers, most of which are related to theological seminaries only for purposes of credit. In the *1984 Yearbook of The American Lutheran Church*, for example, 19 such centers are listed; 25 years ago, few, if any, existed.

As a solution to the stresses and frustrations of the ministry, continuing education opportunities actually kill three birds with one stone: (1) for a few hours each week or for a week at a time, continuing education provides an opportunity to get away for a while from the parish to be with others and, in particular, one's clergy peers; (2) since the courses provided are related directly or indirectly to ministry, the pastor gets new ideas and insights that can stimulate fresh interest in his or her calling; (3) in taking continuing education courses, the pastor returns again to the role of student; the teacher is now the giver. The needed balance is restored.

The balance between giving and receiving is an illustration of the Grubb Theory of Oscillation, developed by Bruce Reed of the Grubb Institute in London, England. According to this theory, people tend to oscillate between two modes of life, extradependence and intradependence. In the intradependent mode, they are dependent on themselves for what they are doing; in the extradependent mode, they are dependent on a source external to themselves. "Strong men," for example, may have a hidden desire at times to be held like a little child by a nurturing parent. During the latter days of my parents' lives, my father, because of the infirmities of age, became increasingly dependent on my mother. When they would visit us, my mother would say to me, "Now he is in your hands!" and she would thoroughly enjoy the freedom from responsibility.

What are the obstacles to such oscillation taking place within the congregational setting? Would not the model of interdependence indigenous to the nature of the church provide the dynamics for this oscillation for the pastor? Is it the priestly function of the clergy that hinders this interdependence? Or is it the executive director function? Or is it a combination of both? For interdependence or oscillation to occur, the "strong one for others" needs to make room for others also to be the strong ones for him or her. In the meantime, continuing education provides one way of getting this needed balance.

Counseling Opportunities for Pastor, Spouse, and Family

While not as many as those favoring the previous solutions, a significant number of questionnaire respondents believe that counseling opportunities for clergy and their families would improve their lot. Many said that it is the responsibility of the denominational synod or district to provide this opportunity. Typical of these is the following: "It is the obligation of church officers and conferences to assist the pastor and his or her family in times of stress."

In spite of this insistence on the responsibility of the church officials to provide counseling opportunities, these church officials themselves, symbolized in the bishop, are in a difficult position to be the "pastor to pastors." Clergy do not believe that the bishop or any other church official is in a position to provide this counseling. They simply cannot believe that counseling with these officials will not affect their call situation. They believe that others believe—and may even believe so themselves—that those who seek and receive help are weaker and therefore less able than those who do not.

Consequently, the commenters tend to recommend that synod or district headquarters make counselors available, both geographically and financially, who are not related in any way to these headquarters. A pastor said, "The threat to job security is real. Therefore, a counselor not related to the call process is imperative." Such a counselor, according to another, would be "a competent person who is unbiased and whom I could trust would not influence church authorities regarding my personal situation."

In my opinion this need for a counselor made available by the church but not reporting to the church is a legitimate concern and request. Even if it were possible that bishops would not be influenced in their thinking regarding call opportunities by their counseling with clergy, the belief that such might be the case is enough to be an obstacle to such counseling. Therefore, church officials need to accept this reality, even though they regret it. (A former bishop noticed that requests for his counsel from his clergy increased noticeably after he announced his retirement.)

When given opportunity to comment on counseling opportunities, 25% did so. Several of those expressed satisfaction with their own regional opportunities. In states where Lutheran Social Service offers counseling to clergy and their families free of charge, the comments regarding this service were positive. Career counseling services made financially available by the church also received appreciation. Some mentioned specific programs operated by the district or conference itself. "We are fortunate in this district," wrote one appreciative pastor, "to have a counseling network for clergy and families." "Our synod clergy support system is ideal," said another. Denominational officials need to share with each other across district, synodical, and even denominational lines what they are doing or are needing to do in regard to making counseling available to clergy and their families. In this way, successful programs can serve as models for the many areas where there is still a need.

A problem as large or even larger than adequate resources for counseling is the openness of the clergy to receive such counseling when they need it. This is the opinion shared by a large number of commenters on this question. Most of these expressed the problem as personal: "The critical factor is how to get me to go, because I am trained to be 'in charge.' Some kind of personal confrontation is probably necessary." This is probably why some commenters want church officials to be aggressive in these matters. "Sources are there," wrote another, "but I am often reluctant to take advantage of them for fear of being 'found' hurting by colleagues/supervisors/congregation." And another, "I need help in asking for help."

Some saw this need as a result of faulty education: "I think pastors should be taught in seminary that they are human and need forgiveness like any other Christian. They and their spouses need to feel the freedom to ask for help when they need it and not feel it is a sign of weakness but of strength and intelligence."

If you are one of these clergy who is reluctant to seek out the help you need because of what you believe it would reveal about you, I would like to reaffirm for you what the above pastor said. It is not a sign of weakness, but of strength and intelligence, for you to ask for counsel. The idea that you are the strong one for others and, therefore, can never need the strength of others is not biblically defensible. It comes from the distorted value system of our culture with its macho-independent/self-sufficient ethos. When this ethos influences also the church, then those who give ministry are conceived as "better" than those who receive it.

Actually, the question of which is better is inconsistent with Christian thinking. You will be a better giver of ministry when you allow yourself to receive it when and where you need it. The biblical view is that receivers are enabled by their receiving to be givers. So, swallow your pride, for that is what it is. Or better, let it die, be crucified with Christ, and in the humility that follows—which is really your strength—ask for help. You will be a better minister to others, as well as a more sensitive person in your family, because of it.

Clinical Pastoral Education

Quite a few pastors in attempting to describe what they felt was needed for improving the lives of clergy referred to some aspect of Clinical Pastoral Education as an example. It is difficult to categorize CPE, because it is both educative, supportive, and therapeutic. In this sense, it combines continuing education with a support group and counseling opportunities. This movement, now organized as the Association of Clinical Pastoral Education, has done much to improve not only the clergy's lot but also the clergy's pastoral skills and, hence, interest in ministry.

Higher Salaries

A sizable majority of respondents believe that higher salaries would improve the lot of clergy. This has long been an acknowledged and legitimate need. Inadequate financial remuneration adds its own stress to an already stressful vocation. Other frustrations are exacerbated by financial problems, especially family irritations. Ultimately these financial problems in a culture such as ours begin to lower our sense of self-esteem. Inadequate remuneration for a pastor, when others in the congregation or even in the district are financially comfortable, is not a Christian balance. It has been demonstrated that the congregation that underpays its clergy is less likely to respect its clergy. Perhaps this is again due to our cultural value system, but it still leads to a vicious cycle.

During a clergy/spouse workshop, a former student of mine and his wife expressed their frustration over his salary. He had accepted a call to a congregation at the minimum salary according to district guidelines. The congregation wanted to have its own pastor rather than share in a two-point parish. However, what they intended to do and what they actually did were two different things. So, after his first year, they cut his salary in order to make ends meet. They did the same thing the second year. The pastor, knowing that the members had been financially devastated by repeated crop failures, doubted that they could do much better. Yet he resented the fact that he had to bear the brunt of their failure. The situation was negatively affecting the couple's attitude toward the congregation, the church, and even their own self-image. While this is not the usual experience of a young pastor, I doubt that it is an isolated incident.

Another irritant in the salary situation is that clergy are often put into the position of having to negotiate their own salary increases, which they thoroughly dislike doing. It does not fit either their own image of the clergy role or what they believe is the laity's view of clergy attitudes toward money. Believing that he was speaking for more than himself, a pastor commented, "I feel one strong contention in the parish ministry is the salary situation. I dislike pastors having to negotiate their own salary!"

I know how he feels. Believing that the congregation should pay something toward my car expense, I emboldened myself to submit such a request in writing (by today's standards, rather modest) to the congregation at its annual meeting, because the proposed budget once again had not included it. I was so uncomfortable about doing so that I chose not to stay for the meeting, which was held immediately after the church service. Instead, my wife and I left immediately to visit friends.

Regardless of whether the image of clergy and money is distorted, others should mediate in these remunerative matters. Someone on the finance committee of the congregation should be so delegated, so that the initiative for reasonable increases for the pastor will be taken. This person would not be seen as a "yes person" to the pastor if he or she were delegated by the congregation to represent the pastor in this matter. Should congregations not take responsible action on the pastor's salary, the district office needs to take its own initiative with such congregations.

One commenter summed it up this way, "What we need is adequate rest and adequate salaries." *Adequate* says it well—but what is an adequate salary in our society?

When I went to Australia, I had no idea of what differences I would find. It turned out that the big difference is in the clergy attitude toward salary. While there, I was informed on several occasions about their practice of paying all clergy the same salary, with added increments for each child in the family. This means that where there is a raise in salary, it is equally distributed. It means that the senior pastor of a large suburban congregation not only gets the same salary as the pastor of a small rural parish or a struggling inner-city congregation but also as the assistant pastor in his own team ministry. It means that the president of the church, the president of the theological seminary, and the seminary graduate in his first call all get the same salary. The Australians that I talked to about this system looked on it as a witness—not to poverty, since they are not poor, but to what a salary should mean.

Even though I knew about this situation, I had thought little of it until I saw that one of the largest contrasts in the entire questionnaire is between the Australian and American clergy attitudes toward salary. In the two variables: "Higher salaries would improve the lot of clergy," and "I do not have enough money to make ends meet," as much as a 30% gap exists between the Australians and both the Americans and Canadians. In contrast to our clergy, Australians do not believe that higher salaries would improve the lot of clergy or that they do not have enough to make ends meet.

This result indicates that while salaries for clergy may be higher proportionately in the United States than in Australia, the system in which salary bears the symbol of status and worth does not produce contentment, even when salaries are increased. Salary for a pastor in Australia is only for receiving an adequate living. The basic needs for livelihood are taken care of by the salary.

Competition and comparison regarding salaries is impossible. In the United States and Canada, the church and its clergy have been influenced by the cultural value system in which the purpose of salary is more than earning a living, because it carries with it a symbolic meaning as well: it is an indicator of how one is valued. One's self-esteem and even self-worth are associated with it. The salary system is thus competitive and comparative.

Such a system actually fosters discontent. Studies have shown that salary in itself does not lead to contentment.[1] As a symbol of how one is doing comparatively, the salary is a reminder that there are those who are doing better, if not in one's own profession, then in some comparable profession, so there is always the push for more. The salary by its comparative nature is extended symbolically into one's standard of living. It should be noted, however, that while the Australian society is similar to that of the United States, it is less competitive.

The salary of the Australian church is "radical" in that it goes back to its *roots*. There are biblical precedents for their salary system. The common treasury of the Jerusalem church is analogous in that all received from it as they had need and none had more or less in possessions. In justifying wages from the congregation to the clergy, St. Paul said, "If we have sown spiritual good among you, is it too much if we reap your material benefits?" (1 Cor. 9:11). But those benefits were obviously to earn a living and not to serve also as cultural status symbols. An American pastor (ALC) suggested this system: "My recommendation is to equalize salaries nationally. The consequence: bigger is no longer better, and small churches would no longer bear an inferiority mentality."

Is such a salary system possible in the United States? Our free-enterprise system is empowered by incentives, and salary increases are perhaps irrevocably yoked with the incentive system. Yet, one can always hope. The proposed merger of the ALC,

LCA, and AELC offers an opportunity for at least a serious consideration of this radical change from the salary-incentive syndrome. From what I have seen of the Australian system and from the results of the questionnaire, I would like to see this tried. It would be a witness for our society and to our laity of values and priorities other than those associated with our comparative, competitive, symbol-oriented remunerative system.

What I have done in this chapter is to permit those who experience the problems to suggest solutions. Receiving insights from the pastors themselves is probably the best way to formulate answers. Perhaps the questionnaire had a midwife role in drawing out these ideas. In any case, I was impressed by the cumulative wisdom that came forth.

For Your Doing

Individual

1. What are your stressors? How could your lot be improved for you? Mark your responses on parts D, E, and F of the questionnaire in Appendix A and compare your results with those reported in the research. How do you compare to the research findings? Any clues about your situation that help explain the difference—if there is one?
2. Write a definition of *stress* and *distress*. Are they the same or different? What transforms *stress* into *distress* in your life?
3. Who are the role senders (persons who have expectations of others) in your personal, family, and professional life? Write the name of persons or situations and identify the particular expectations. Are you surprised by your list? Did you place your own name on the list?

With Others

1. Read a time-management book (*The Time Trap* by R. Alec Mackenzie [McGraw-Hill, 1975] is a good one) and discuss its implications with your executive or support committee.

2. Set up your own local continuing education group by selecting a topic and group members that meet your particular needs. Write SELECT, 2199 East Main Street, Columbus, Ohio 43209, for details on courses and group information. SELECT is an inter-Lutheran continuing education center.

For Denominational Leaders

1. When and where do pastors learn the practical side of parish ministry? Should the seminaries expand their curriculum? Could seminary graduates be better guided into pastoral ministry? Is learning by trial and error too expensive for new pastors and congregations?
2. It is time for congregations to add staff, since buildings are now being paid off. Help your agencies dream new staff possibilities.
3. Part-time pastoral ministry is a way for some congregations to have and/or add staff. Check with your churchwide staff to see what resources are available to support this growing ministry.
4. Encourage congregations to provide two days off per week for professionals. Sabbaticals are also most useful for renewal.
5. Sabbatical model:
   a. Policy
      —Three to six months for each six years of service.
      —One year of continued service following.
      —January to August better than September to January.
      —A specific sabbatical plan developed and approved by the congregation.
   b. Finances
      —Congregation pays financial support for educational costs to equal three years of continuing education dollars, full salary continues.
      —Pastor pays transportation and any additional living costs in sabbatical location.

—District/synod make a financial contribution to cover pastoral supply for worship and emergency ministries.

c. Program

—Important to have a change of scene.

—Opportunity for personal, professional, and family enrichment.

—Educational goals that can be implemented in the life and mission of the congregation.

d. Parish Leadership

—Develop leadership plan to avoid overload of other staff.

—Clarify assignments of leadership staff.

—Write out sabbatical agreement together with the pastor in as full detail as possible.

7

Conclusion:
For Improved Health
of Parish Ministry

Summary Observations from the Data

Four subgroups of Lutheran clergy have similar but not identical profiles: those who (1) are dissatisfied with their spiritual/devotional life; (2) definitely agree that their life-style makes them a high risk for a heart attack; (3) report "conflicts with congregation" as a source of somewhat to very serious stress; and (4) are hurting badly as judged by their written comments. The four opposite groups also have similar but not identical *contrasting* profiles: those who (1) are not dissatisfied with their spiritual/devotional life; (2) definitely disagree that their life-style makes them a high risk for a heart attack; (3) report no stress from "conflicts with congregation"; and (4) are feeling great.

The first of these four contrasting pairs (satisfied versus dissatisfied with spiritual/devotional life) differ in terms of the largest number of survey items (123 items of 270, or 46%). The second pair (at risk versus not at risk) differ next most (116 items, or 43%). The third pair (stressed versus not stressed from conflict) differ next most (93 items, or 34%). And the fourth pair (hurting versus feeling great) differ in terms of the smallest number of specific survey items (44 items, or 16%). However, this does not mean that the fourth pair (hurting versus feeling great) are least distinct from each other, for they were initially distinguished by their unusual replies when asked to comment on the health of contemporary parish ministry. Both groups commented, but what they commented on were their own lives and ministries in such ways as to demonstrate unmistakably the fact that they were either hurting badly or feeling great.

The profiles óf the first two pairs (dissatisfied with spiritual/ devotional life and at risk of heart attack) are the most similar of the four (84 contrasts in common). This may be in part because those who see themselves as at risk of a heart attack also are inclined to be dissatisfied with their spiritual/devotional lives.

The third (in conflict with the congregation) is less similar but about equally similar to each of the first two (dissatisfied with spiritual/devotional life and at risk) with 55 and 54 contrasts in common.

And the fourth (hurting) is still less similar but about equally with each of the other three (37, 32, and 33 contrasts in common, respectively).

Therefore, those dissatisfied with their spiritual/devotional lives and those who consider themselves at risk of heart attack are most alike. Those stressed due to conflict share about half of what the dissatisfied and at risk have in common. Those hurting badly are least like the other three. Nevertheless, the dissatisfied, at risk, and conflicted each share at least three-fourths of all the things discovered in this study that distinguish those who hurt from those who feel great.

Interpretation and Reflections

While these four subgroups have varying affinities with each other, their common characteristics are preponderant. Since they reflect groups both around negative characteristics as well as around their positive opposites, they are in essence a data summary or conclusion to this study. Since we initiated the study to determine the state of health of the parish ministry, we find that this question is closely related to the health of the parish pastor. As one of our commenters aptly perceived, "Improving the parish ministry centers mostly in improving the minister."

The variants in the four subgroupings indicate implicitly how to improve the health of the parish pastor. This improvement is focused in three areas, in order of data preponderance: (1) the need for clergy care; (2) the need for more effective structuring of relationships of clergy with their congregation, family, and clergy peers; (3) the need for more lay participation in ministry. The suggestions for improving the health of the parish ministry by clergy who wrote comments group together in these same three areas.

The Need for Clergy Self-Care

The concern that clergy life-style makes them a high risk for a heart attack sets the tone for clergy care. The life-style that predisposes to a heart attack is one characterized by stress, specifically *distress*. Stress, in turn, is predisposed by an imbalance in one's distribution of time and energy to the neglect of pursuits and functions associated with healthy living. Because of the specific dimensions or natures that constitute human nature, any life-style that persistently ignores any of these is imbalanced. The human person has spiritual, physical, socio-emotional, and mental dimensions, and balance occurs when the person responds to the need of each dimension.

M. Scott Peck defines such balancing as a discipline, because it involves the experience of giving up something to which one has become attached. He describes his own painful experience of giving up the need to win, which was consuming most of his time and energy and shaping his priorities.[1] A similar discipline for clergy seeking balance could be giving up the need to be a perfect pastor, parent, or spouse. The balance is restored as one gives up this drive that pressures one to be a professional "loner," and joins with the imperfect people of the extended family of the church. Groups that provide for intimacy with family and friends help one achieve this balance.

Because work becomes the principal imbalancing factor in one's efforts to be the perfect pastor, balancing also means giving up some of the time and energy given to work and devoting it to other interests and hobbies that stimulate the mind. Continuing education programs and sabbaticals play their significant roles in assisting clergy to achieve this balance in their living.

To reduce the risk of heart attack, one needs antidotes to stress. One such antidote is doing what needs to be done to achieve a realistic workload. This also is a discipline—the creaturely discipline of accepting limits. Another antidote comes from the spiritual and physical exercise involved in achieving a balanced lifestyle. Psychiatrist William Glasser called physical exercise (specifically, running) and spiritual exercise (specifically, meditation) the two most positive addictions. Rather than referring to them as addictions, I would prefer to call them two of the more rewarding pursuits for balance for those with tension-related jobs.

According to the questionnaire data and, in particular, these concluding subgroupings, a satisfying devotional life appears to be pivotal for achieving the positive characteristics of the subgroupings. As a companion pursuit, regular physical exercise has long been known as a stress reducer. One of our commenters at age 63 wrote, "I am a firm believer in daily exercise. I play an hour of tennis five days a week. This truly helps my outlook on life." Significantly, the data show that those who are dissatisfied with their devotional life tend also to be dissatisfied with the appearance of their bodies. These interrelationships both at the negative and positive ends of these subgroups are an affirmation of a holistic perception of human nature.

Clergy care is a corporate effort of clergy and the laity of the congregation. It is difficult for clergy to care for themselves if their congregations are uncooperative and unsympathetic. At the same time, it is only as the clergy themselves take this responsibility for their care that such care is likely to take place.

Taking care of others does not preclude taking care of oneself, but may in fact depend on it. Some clergy tend to confuse their calling with the need to drive and sacrifice themselves, subjugating their own self-interests to the interests of others. Some might even confuse this kind of self-abnegation with the cross that is laid on them as Christ's symbol bearers. The cross, however, means accepting the sufferings that come from one's faithfulness to his or her witness; it is the price one may pay for being a true prophet.

Jesus met his spiritual and emotional needs by retreating to the deserts, the mountains, the lonely places. Sometimes he went by himself; at other times he took his disciples with him. He climbed mountains for the right atmosphere for prayer, exercising not only his spirit but his body. He walked through Judea, Samaria, and Galilee. Sometimes he did what people asked him to, and sometimes he did not. Taking care of his needs in this way helped him to take up his cross.

Taking care of ourselves, as Jesus did, helps us to be more open to the Spirit's guidance and, hence, more perceptive in recognizing our cross. Otherwise, our unmet needs will get projected into our supposed sacrificing and serving and inhibit our ability to give of ourselves—to love—even if we give away all that we have or deliver our bodies to be burned (1 Cor. 13:3). For this reason, when we do take care of ourselves, not only we but our congregations, family, and friends will be the beneficiaries.

The Need for More Effective Structuring of Relationships with the Congregation

More effective structuring of relationships pertains directly to the clergy's need for conflict-management skills. It is doubtful whether there is anything more stressful in parish ministry than interpersonal conflicts with the people of the congregation. "I believe the greatest area for growth,'' wrote a pastor, ''is in knowing how to handle conflict within oneself, family, and congregation.'' Since a community goes with the job, how best can its systems be organized so that they function with the least stress and most effectiveness? What kind of clergy/lay structures can the pastor live with most positively?

The answer to these questions must include the recognition, clarification, and affirmation of boundaries between obligations to the congregation, to one's family, and to one's own person. Such clarification is best achieved through the process of consensus among those involved and is best affirmed by the pastor when he or she is also flexible and sensitive.

Positively speaking, such effective structuring is a matter of actualizing the potential of the systems inherent in the congregation as an extended family community. Effective structuring provides the opportunity for both clergy and laity to take the initiative in knowing, caring for, and enjoying the other members of the body. It is through such systems of intimacy that ministry can best take place. These systems of intimacy need also to be extended to one's clergy peers so that competitive isolation can be overcome by cooperative caring. This would clear these systems of obstacles to support and friendship.

One of the commenters believed the best way to achieve this effective structuring in the congregation is through pastoral visitation. ''Be zealous in home visitation,'' he wrote, ''because there the pastor has the best opportunity of applying the gospel to the individual—as well as listening to his or her hurts and joys.'' The aim of such house visitation is good, but I believe as a methodology it is dated. In some parishes, routine visiting is neither feasible nor advisable. Many people in today's society do not relish being interrupted, even by a pastoral visit. They have their work plans or recreation plans and are under time pressures like the pastor. Although there are exceptional instances, a routine visitation program to the homes of parishioners may not even be a good stewardship of time.

It is more effective for ministry to visit when there is an obvious need—or a specific purpose—or when invited or requested to do so for a specific reason or occasion. Otherwise, we need to cultivate a more effective way for maintaining and deepening our contacts with people. One possibility is to take advantage of all gatherings, chance encounters, and even committee meetings to listen to people and to show a personal interest in them. I have discovered that going early to gatherings—or staying late—provides good opportunities for casual conversations as people wait to gather, which with good listening can become meaningful encounters.

This effective structuring of relationships is obviously a mutual effort of clergy and laity. Lay persons also need to make overtures for caring and knowing—to each other and to clergy and to clergy families. Many of us find it difficult to make such overtures, because the timing may not be right for the other. It is hard on our self-esteem to be turned down. Still we need to give the other this opportunity to say yes or no. One of the most infuriating statements is, "We didn't know whether you'd be interested, and so we didn't ask you." More effective structuring of relationships makes possible a mutuality of ministry—or what the Scripture calls "mutual upbuilding" (Rom. 14:19). This leads us to the third of these areas for improvement.

The Need for More Lay Participation in Ministry

Because there are so many opportunities for ministry in congregations and conscientious clergy find it difficult to leave any of them unrealized, the more lay persons participate in these ministries, the less stress the clergy may experience. More work gets done when more people are involved. It should be said, however, that lay workers who feel unsupported and taken for granted can burn out in their work for the church and become "turned off" to the church. They too need to be protected from the tensions of overload.

Clergy have a strong sense of need for this lay participation but they apparently also need assistance in learning how to catalyze it. "The need of our church," wrote a pastor, "is to develop means by which to train lay leadership." When clergy become more skilled in catalyzing lay participation, rather than being one of their least satisfying ministries, it will become one of their most satisfying.

These skills center in a particular style of leadership. Some leaders assume so much authority that they leave little room for others to assume any. Other leaders are so lacking in authority that they leave the lay people with no sense of direction in which to assume authority. Clergy who catalyze lay participation are those who retain the authority of their offices and yet share it with others. Theirs is a dialectical approach to authority in which they stay in control and yet surrender that control when in trust they work together with others. They use the symbolic role of their office to stimulate and inspire this involvement of others. They use the equipping-for-ministry function of their office within the interdependency model of the body of Christ. Not only does this style of leadership catalyze lay participation, it produces a positive stress for the clergy. It is actually exciting to see the results of this ministry in the involvement of lay people in love and care for others.

Clergy may also need assistance in dealing with the potential threat that increased lay participation may bring. Some may not be aware that they are potentially threatened by lay involvement and, as a result, may subconsciously enable *non*participation, even as they complain about it. This is a typical behavior pattern of enablers, whether of chemical dependency or lay apathy. What they significantly omit in their approach is positive reinforcement. Instead, they resort to the accusatory law and lament, complain or scold—with exactly the results that they anticipate and may even subconsciously need.

Once we can face and accept the threat of sharing our authority and control with lay persons, we can let the gospel motivate our approach. Accepting people as they are, we can listen to them and help them to formulate their ideas and put them into service. Besides adding to the core of congregational workers, such an approach lessens the work load of the clergy, while at the same time enhancing the scope of their ministry. It also adds to the vocational fulfillment of the lay persons. Their participation in the ministry of the congregation is their own response to the call of God. Their participation also increases their sense of belonging in the congregation. As they accept their *responsibility* in the life of this extended family, they will experience the *support* of this family. Theirs is a participation in line with the doctrine of the church as a body of mutually related members. Through their participation, they are contributing to the health of this body, since this health is contained in the healthy systems of the membership.

The parish ministry is basic to most other ministries of the church. The church as worshiping congregations provides the means for the church to engage in the great majority of specialized ministries, including teaching in theological seminaries and administering in denominational headquarters. The health of the parish and its ministry is basic to the health of the church in all its ministries.

Guidelines for Self-care

Below you will find a survey of health habits that promote self-care. Respond to the questions as honestly as possible, and then read the interpretation and follow the reflection guide.

Health Habit Inventory

Yes	No	*Physical*
___	___	I participate regularly (three times a week or more) in a vigorous physical exercise program.
___	___	I eat a well-balanced diet.

_____ _____ My weight is within 10 pounds of the ideal weight for my height.

_____ _____ My alcohol consumption is seven drinks (shot, beer, or glass of wine) or fewer per week.

_____ _____ I always wear my seat belt.

_____ _____ I do not smoke cigarettes, cigars, or a pipe.

_____ _____ I generally get adequate and satisfying sleep.

Mental

_____ _____ I seldom experience periods of depression.

_____ _____ I generally face up to problems and cope with change effectively.

_____ _____ I worry very little about future possibilities or things I can't change.

_____ _____ I laugh several times a day and usually fit "play" into my schedule.

_____ _____ I am curious and always on the lookout for new learning.

_____ _____ I maintain a realistic and basically positive self-image.

_____ _____ I choose to feel confident and optimistic.

Relational

_____ _____ I seek help and support when I need it.

_____ _____ I have at least one friend with whom I can share almost anything.

_____ _____ I have nourishing intimate relationships with family and/or friends.

_____ _____ I experience and express a wide range of emotions and respond to others' feelings appropriately.

_____ _____ Each day includes a comfortable and stimulating interaction with others, frequently new acquaintances.

_____ _____ I solicit and accept feedback from others.

_____ _____ I stick up for myself when it's necessary and appropriate.

Spiritual

_____ _____ I set aside 15–20 minutes each day for prayer or meditation.

_____ _____ I participate in regular spiritual rituals with people who share my beliefs.

_____ _____ I accept my limitations and inadequacies without embarrassment or apology.

_____ _____ I keep the purpose of my life clearly in mind and let it guide my goal setting and decision making.

_____ _____ I regularly offer my time and possessions in service to others.

_____ _____ I am sensitive to ultimate truths and the spiritual dimension of life.

_____ _____ I readily forgive myself and others.

Physical	_____	Yes responses
Mental	_____	Yes responses
Relational	_____	Yes responses
Spiritual	_____	Yes responses
Total	_____	Out of 28 questions

How to Interpret Your Score

Your total of yes responses of the Health Habit Inventory provides a general idea of how well you take care of your health across all dimensions of life. Compare your total score to the Caring Question Standards:

24-28—Excellent: Your health habits are enhancing your health.
16-23—Average: You're obviously trying, but there's room for improvement.

Below 16—Poor: The quality of your health is probably diminished by your poor habits.

For specifics on your self-care, pay particular attention to your score in each of the four categories: physical, mental, relational, and spiritual. If you recorded three or fewer yes responses in any dimension, you're neglecting your health in that area. If you aren't yet experiencing symptoms, you probably will soon.

In those areas where you answered yes four or five times, you're probably taking adequate care of yourself. Your self-care habits do enhance your health, but you might consider upgrading some for optimal healthfulness. There's still room for improvement.

Yes responses to six or seven questions in any category indicates that you are practicing self-care habits. Congratulations! Over the long run your choices will enhance the quality of your life and your health.

Take a few minutes to reflect on your score and your reactions to it. Use the worksheet below to record your insights and resolutions for change.

Personal Reflection on My Self-Care Patterns

In which areas are your habits an asset? _____

_____

In which areas are your habits a liability? _____

_____

In which areas would you like to make changes? _____

_____

_____

Which particular habits would you like to modify? _____

_____

From Donald and Nancy Tubesing, *The Caring Question*
(Minneapolis: Augsburg, 1983)

APPENDIX A

The Questionnaire:
What's Happening in Pastoral
Ministry?

1. Sex and clergy status (*check one*).

   _____ Male clergy

   _____ Male-clergy's spouse

   _____ Male clergy and female-clergy's spouse

   _____ Female clergy

   _____ Female-clergy's spouse

   _____ Female clergy and male-clergy's spouse

2. Age _____

3. Church body:

   _____ ALC

   _____ LCA

   _____ LC–MS

   _____ Other (specify)

4. Marital status (check one):

   _____ Never married

   _____ Married

   _____ Separated

   _____ Divorced

   _____ Widowed

5. If ever married, and had one or more children, indicate present family status (*check one*).

_____ Beginning family (oldest child less than 30 months)

_____ Family with preschool children (oldest 30 months–6 years)

_____ Family with school children (oldest 6–13 years)

_____ Family with teenagers (oldest 13–20 or so years)

_____ Family as launching center (first child gone to last child leaving)

_____ Family in middle years (empty nest to retirement)

_____ Aging family (in retirement)

6. If clergy spouse, are you employed for pay? _____ Yes _____ No

7. If yes, _____ Part-time _____ Full-time

8. If yes, how satisfied with work? _____ Very _____ Somewhat _____ Not

9. If clergy, how many years in ordained ministry? _____

10. (*check one*)
If clergy, please describe your present ministry (or ministry of your spouse, if you are not clergy).

_____ Solo pastor

_____ Associate or Assistant

_____ Copastor

_____ Senior Pastor

_____ Chaplain

_____ Educator

_____ Administrator

_____ Other specialized ministry

11. (*check one*)

_____ One congregation

_____ More than one congregation

_____ Agency or institution

12. (*check one*)

_____ United States

_____ Other country: _____

Please continue describing present ministry. Check one location for each congregation you now serve.

13. Cong. One	14. Cong. Two	15. Cong. Three	16. Cong. Four	
———	———	———	———	Inner city of metropolis over 1,000,000
———	———	———	———	Urban area of metropolis
———	———	———	———	Suburb of metropolis
———	———	———	———	Center of large city (250,000 to 1,000,000)
———	———	———	———	Urban area of large city
———	———	———	———	Suburb of large city
———	———	———	———	Center of medium city (50,000–250,000)
———	———	———	———	Urban area of medium city
———	———	———	———	Suburb of medium city
———	———	———	———	Small city (10,000–50,000)
———	———	———	———	Town (2500–10,000)
———	———	———	———	Rural town (under 2500)
———	———	———	———	Rural or farm (open country)

Personal Satisfaction

A. Activities that I feel positive about in my ministry:
(If you are not clergy, but a spouse of clergy, please give your perception of how that clergy person feels about these activities in his or her ministry.)

(For each activity, circle one number.)	Not Positive				Most Positive
17. Preaching	1	2	3	4	5
18. Counseling	1	2	3	4	5
19. Teaching (adult)	1	2	3	4	5
20. Confirmation	1	2	3	4	5

21.	Administration	1	2	3	4	5
22.	Community responsibility	1	2	3	4	5
23.	Prophetic witness	1	2	3	4	5
24.	Youth work	1	2	3	4	5
25.	Ministry with aged	1	2	3	4	5
26.	Worship leading	1	2	3	4	5
27.	Specialized group work	1	2	3	4	5
28.	Evangelism	1	2	3	4	5
29.	Sick visitation	1	2	3	4	5

B-1. How satisfied/dissatisfied are you with your:
(If you are not clergy, but a spouse of clergy, please give your perception of how that clergy person feels.)

(Check one answer for each.)	Very Satisfied	Satisfied	So-so	Dissatisfied	Very Dissatisfied
30. Sense of personal accomplishment?	____	____	____	____	____
31. Nurturing support from the congregation?	____	____	____	____	____
32. Opportunities for advancement?	____	____	____	____	____
33. Respect and status in the community?	____	____	____	____	____
34. Freedom to carry out ministry as you understand it?	____	____	____	____	____
35. Sense of doing something of value?	____	____	____	____	____
36. Recognition by officers of congregation or district?	____	____	____	____	____
37. Distribution of own time and energy?	____	____	____	____	____
38. Spouse's close identification with your work?	____	____	____	____	____
39. Use of your talents?	____	____	____	____	____

40. Opportunity for balanced living—including time for self?	___	___	___	___	___
41. Sensing of God's direction in your work?	___	___	___	___	___
42. Competency in your work?	___	___	___	___	___
43. Faithfulness to your sense of calling?	___	___	___	___	___
44. Personal prayer life?	___	___	___	___	___
45. Family devotional life?	___	___	___	___	___
46. Devotions with spouse?	___	___	___	___	___
47. Relationships with staff and professional co-workers?	___	___	___	___	___
48. Sense of satisfaction with your ministry?	___	___	___	___	___

B-2 If dissatisfied with any of these, what is it due to?
(*Circle one letter for each. If satisfied, leave blank.*)
a. time factor
b. energy factor
c. lack of cooperation of others
d. own lack of motivation
e. own lack of initiative
f. lack of clarity as to what you want

49. Faithfulness to your sense of calling	a b c d e f
50. Personal prayer life	a b c d e f
51. Family devotional life	a b c d e f
52. Devotions with spouse	a b c d e f
53. Sense of satisfaction with your ministry	a b c d e f

C. When you participate in them, which three of these give you the greatest satisfaction? (Rank them first, second, and third by writing 1, 2, and 3 in the blanks beside them.) Which one gives you the least satisfaction? (Rank that last by writing 9 in the blank beside it.) Write only 1, 2, 3, and 9.

_____ 54. Group recreational activities

_____ 55. Friendship

_____ 56. Time alone for myself (hobbies, etc.)

_____ 57. Time alone with my spouse

_____ 58. Time alone with my family

_____ 59. Full- or part-time studies

_____ 60. Physical exercise

_____ 61. To stimulate lay ministry

_____ 62. Community service

_____ 63. Other (please specify): _____

64. Overall, how would you rate your satisfaction with regard to fulfillment of your own personal goals and self-development?

_____ Very satisfactory

_____ Satisfactory

_____ Satisfactory and unsatisfactory, or unsure

_____ Unsatisfactory

_____ Very unsatisfactory

65. Overall, how would you describe your present relationship with your congregation?

_____ Very satisfactory

_____ Satisfactory

_____ Satisfactory and unsatisfactory, or unsure

_____ Unsatisfactory

_____ Very unsatisfactory

66. Overall, how would you describe your relationship with your spouse?

_____ Very satisfactory

_____ Satisfactory

_____ Satisfactory and unsatisfactory, or unsure

_____ Unsatisfactory

_____ Very unsatisfactory

67. Overall, how would you rate the health of contemporary parish ministry?

_____ Very satisfactory

_____ Satisfactory

_____ Satisfactory and unsatisfactory, or unsure

_____ Unsatisfactory

_____ Very unsatisfactory

Stress

D. Please indicate the extent to which any of these is a source of stress for you and your family (or you alone, if not married). If spouse, answer for self, and omit items 75 and 85.

Very Serious Stress	Somewhat Serious Stress	No Stress	
68. _____	_____	_____	Time pressures
69. _____	_____	_____	Income
70. _____	_____	_____	Housing
71. _____	_____	_____	Lack of mobility
72. _____	_____	_____	Too great mobility
73. _____	_____	_____	Lack of social life/friends
74. _____	_____	_____	Community pressure on children
75. _____	_____	_____	Spouse regarded as pastoral extension
76. _____	_____	_____	Dual careers
77. _____	_____	_____	Lack of employment opportunities for spouse
78. _____	_____	_____	Privacy needs
79. _____	_____	_____	Conflicts with congregation
80. _____	_____	_____	Conflicts with spouse
81. _____	_____	_____	Conflicts with own children
82. _____	_____	_____	Role expectations of self and others
83. _____	_____	_____	Frustration in conforming to expectations
84. _____	_____	_____	Spiritual/devotional life

85. _____ _____   _____ Other clergy's jealousy of your talents
86. _____ _____   _____ Loneliness/isolation
87. _____ _____   _____ Unfair treatment by parishioners
88. _____ _____   _____ Physical health problems
89. _____ _____   _____ Poor educational opportunities for children
90. _____ _____   _____ Lack of cultural opportunities
91. _____ _____   _____ Frustration in carrying out ministry as you view it
92. _____ _____   _____ Other (please specify): _____

E. How frequently do you *think about behaving* or *actually behave* in the following ways? (Circle one for each.)
   F = Frequently
   O = Occasionally
   N = Never or very rarely

	Thoughts	Behavior
a. Suicide	(93) F O N	(100) F O N
b. Self-sabotaging behavior	(94) F O N	(101) F O N
c. Giving spouse or family "the silent treatment"	(95) F O N	(102) F O N
d. Infidelity	(96) F O N	(103) F O N
e. Excessive use of alcohol or other drugs	(97) F O N	(104) F O N
f. Own or spouse's resignation from ministry	(98) F O N	(105) F O N
g. Divorce	(99) F O N	(106) F O N

107. Which period of your ministry would you say placed the greatest stress on you? (*Check one.*)

(1) _____ First year   (5) _____ 16-20 years   (9) _____ Other
(2) _____ 2-5 years   (6) _____ 21-25 years   (Please specify):
(3) _____ 6-10 years   (7) _____ After 25 years
(4) _____ 11-15 years   (8) _____ Retirement years   (10) _____ None

Improvements

F. Which of the following do you feel would improve the lot of clergy in general? (*Check as many as apply.*)

_____ 108. Higher salaries

_____ 109. Improved church headquarters' understanding of the ministry

_____ 110. Clergy-family retreats and workshops

_____ 111. Training Ministerial Relations committees to work with clergy and their spouses

_____ 112. Opportunities for continuing education for pastors and their spouses

_____ 113. Clarification of professional standards/protection of pastors from subjective evaluations

_____ 114. Counseling for clergy families

_____ 115. Opportunity for more contact with other clergy couples

_____ 116. Better support from denomination, district, or synod

_____ 117. More support for clergy in disputes between clergy and congregation

_____ 118. Babysitting and childcare allowances

_____ 119. More opportunities for moving

_____ 120. Income adequate enough to purchase a home

_____ 121. Other (please specify): _____

G. When or if you were to have personal problems, to whom do or would you turn for help? From the list below, choose the three *most likely* and number them I, 2, and 3. Number the *least likely* with a 9. (Rank only 1, 2, 3, and 9.)

_____ 122. A member of your congregation

_____ 123. A friend outside the congregation

_____ 124. Your spouse (or significant other)

_____ 125. A relative

_____ 126. A pastor of your own denomination

_____ 127. A pastor in another denomination

_____ 128. Your physician

_____ 129. Your bishop

_____ 130. A clinically trained pastor

_____ 131. A psychiatrist or psychologist

_____ 132. No one

_____ 133. Other (please specify): _____

134. Do you feel there is a need for better sources of help in time of personal troubles? _____ Yes _____ No _____ Not sure

135. Comments:

Detailed Concerns

H. These statements describe things which sometimes trouble people, or which people may spend a great deal of time thinking about. First, on the *left* side of the page: Show how much you *agree or disagree* with each by circling one of these answers:

SA = Strongly agree   TD = Tend to disagree

A = Agree   D = Disagree

TA = Tend to agree   SD = Strongly disagree

Second, on the *right* side of the page: Show how much you are *bothered* by each by circling one of these answers:

N (Never) I am not bothered by this and I never have been; (or) this does not apply to my situation, or has not been part of my experience.
NL (No longer) This used to bother me, but it doesn't any more.
V (Very much) This bothers me a lot.
Q (Quite a bit) This bothers me less than "a lot," but still quite a bit.
S (Somewhat) This bothers me somewhat.
L (Very little) This bothers me only a little.

As you read each statement think, "How much am I bothered by this?" Don't spend too long trying to decide precisely how much a thing bothers you; just circle your first reaction to the statement and go on to the next.

(136) SA A TA TD D SD	I feel the competitive pressure with brother and sister pastors to the point that it is difficult to be open and vulnerable with them.	N NL V Q S L (194)
(137) SA A TA TD D SD	I am inclined to put off dealing with irritations and conflict.	N NL V Q S L (195)

(138) SA A TA TD D SD   I am inclined to stuff my   N NL V Q S L (196)
                             feelings rather than ex-
                             press them directly.

(139) SA A TA TD D SD   I am inclined to blow   N NL V Q S L (197)
                             up—lose my temper—
                             rather than maintain a
                             reasoned approach.

(140) SA A TA TD D SD   I feel more comfortable   N NL V Q S L (198)
                             with men than women in
                             my ministry.

(141) SA A TA TD D SD   I feel more comfortable   N NL V Q S L (199)
                             with women than men in
                             my ministry.

(142) SA A TA TD D SD   I find it difficult to confront N NL V Q S L (200)
                             people with their moral
                             and ethical responsibili-
                             ties.

(143) SA A TA TD D SD   I feel inadequate or even   N NL V Q S L (201)
                             hypocritical in being a
                             pastor.

(144) SA A TA TD D SD   Stress in my marriage af-   N NL V Q S L (202)
                             fects my ministry ad-
                             versely—makes me feel
                             inadequate for ministry.

(145) SA A TA TD D SD   I have self-doubts about   N NL V Q S L (203)
                             my competency for min-
                             istry.

(146) SA A TA TD D SD   There is sufficient com-   N NL V Q S L (204)
                             munication with my con-
                             gregation for me to
                             receive the feedback I
                             need to evaluate my min-
                             istry.

(147) SA A TA TD D SD   Husbands and wives   N NL V Q S L (205)
                             should share responsi-
                             bility for household du-
                             ties.

(148) SA A TA TD D SD   Before a difficult day, I   N NL V Q S L (206)
                             usually find it hard to
                             sleep because of being
                             preoccupied with anxie-
                             ty.

(149) SA A TA TD D SD   After a hectic day it's usually impossible for me to keep from replaying in my mind things that happened.   N NL V Q S L (207)

(150) SA A TA TD D SD   A mother should have primary responsibility for the care and nurture of children.   N NL V Q S L (208)

(151) SA A TA TD D SD   The quality of our marriage and family life (were it known) provides poor witness to the congregation/community.   N NL V Q S L (209)

(152) SA A TA TD D SD   I find life exciting and full of fun.   N NL V Q S L (210)

(153) SA A TA TD D SD   People who know me well agree that I take my work too seriously.   N NL V Q S L (211)

(154) SA A TA TD D SD   I feel my future is bright.   N NL V Q S L (212)

(155) SA A TA TD D SD   I get into moods where I can't seem to cheer up.   N NL V Q S L (213)

(156) SA A TA TD D SD   My feelings are easily hurt.   N NL V Q S L (214)

(157) SA A TA TD D SD   I find it very difficult to speak on social issues because of possible controversy.   N NL V Q S L (215)

(158) SA A TA TD D SD   Most of the time, I am free from tension and frustration.   N NL V Q S L (216)

(159) SA A TA TD D SD   I can turn people down, say no, or otherwise decline others in giving priority to my own needs without feeling guilty.   N NL V Q S L (217)

(160) SA A TA TD D SD   A woman's career should be secondary to her husband's.   N NL V Q S L (218)

(161) SA A TA TD D SD

Some equality in marriage is a good thing, but by and large the husband ought to have the final word in family matters.

N NL V Q S L (219)

(162) SA A TA TD D SD

My spouse and I are unable to quarrel constructively to resolve our conflicts.

N NL V Q S L (220)

(163) SA A TA TD D SD

I wish I were more efficient in my work.

N NL V Q S L (221)

(164) SA A TA TD D SD

It seems that societal values rather than those of the gospel influence the way congregations and pastors evaluate success or failure.

N NL V Q S L (222)

(165) SA A TA TD D SD

I often think I could serve God better outside the parish ministry.

N NL V Q S L (223)

(166) SA A TA TD D SD

I cannot live up to the standards I set for myself.

N NL V Q S L (224)

(167) SA A TA TD D SD

I do not have enough money to make ends meet.

N NL V Q S L (225)

(168) SA A TA TD D SD

Because of being a single person, I do not feel accepted by my congregation.

N NL V Q S L (226)

(169) SA A TA TD D SD

I get little help from my spouse in running the household.

N NL V Q S L (227)

(170) SA A TA TD D SD

My spouse does not spend enough time with our children.

N NL V Q S L (228)

(171) SA A TA TD D SD

I wonder whether my sexual desire is adequate.

N NL V Q S L (229)

(172) SA A TA TD D SD

Some members of my family do not attend worship services.

N NL V Q S L (230)

(173) SA A TA TD D SD   I feel pressured to get a job.   N NL V Q S L (231)

(174) SA A TA TD D SD   I may not have enough financial security for retirement.   N NL V Q S L (232)

(175) SA A TA TD D SD   I feel unable to cope with my children.   N NL V Q S L (233)

(176) SA A TA TD D SD   I can't communicate with my spouse.   N NL V Q S L (234)

(177) SA A TA TD D SD   I am frequently torn between conflicting values, beliefs, and desires.   N NL V Q S L (235)

(178) SA A TA TD D SD   I do not feel good about the appearance of my body.   N NL V Q S L (236)

(179) SA A TA TD D SD   My drinking may become a problem.   N NL V Q S L (237)

(180) SA A TA TD D SD   Some of my children are living a life-style which I do not approve.   N NL V Q S L (238)

(181) SA A TA TD D SD   I feel guilt and disappointment over my performance as a parent.   N NL V Q S L (239)

(182) SA A TA TD D SD   My spiritual life is in trouble.   N NL V Q S L (240)

(183) SA A TS TD D SD   My spouse is not as sexually interested in me as I would like.   N NL V Q S L (241)

(184) SA A TA TD D SD   I feel angry, frustrated, or tense far too much of the time.   N NL V Q S L (242)

(185) SA A TA TD D SD   I often feel that everything I do is an effort.   N NL V Q S L (243)

(186) SA A TA TD D SD   I am too anxious to please others.   N NL V Q S L (244)

(187) SA A TA TD D SD   I am getting old.   N NL V Q S L (245)

(188) SA A TA TD D SD   I wonder whether my sexual desires are normal.   N NL V Q S L (246)

(189) SA A TA TD D SD   My life-style makes me a high risk for a heart attack.   N NL V Q S L (247)

(190) SA A TA TD D SD	Society seems to value success so much more than service.	N NL V Q S L (248)
(191) SA A TA TD D SD	My church body seems to value success like society does.	N NL V Q S L (249)
(192) SA A TA TD D SD	I feel uncomfortable about compromises I have made with my calling as God's spokesperson.	N NL V Q S L (250)
(193) SA A TA TD D SD	I like my work.	N NL V Q S L (251)

Pastor's Spouse in the Congregation

I. To what extent do *you* and the *members of your congregation* agree or disagree with each of the following statements about the role of the pastor's spouse in the congregation? Using the code that follows, insert in the left column before *each* statement the single number which *most* adequately reflects *your* opinion (in the right column, the *congregation's* opinion). When you are finished, each space should have a number on it.

Code:
5 = Strongly agree
4 = Agree
3 = Equally agree or disagree, or not sure
2 = Disagree
1 = Strongly disagree

My   Congregation's
Opinion   Opinion
_____

The pastor's spouse should:

252. ____ 261. ____   be deeply involved in the life of the congregation.

253. ____ 262. ____   have an equal opportunity to choose church membership or nonmembership.

254. ___ 263. ___   have an equal right as a member of a congregation to be considered for election to leadership.

255. ___ 264. ___   always publicly be supportive of spouse's ministry.

256. ___ 265. ___   take a leadership role in the congregation beyond that of most other lay persons.

257. ___ 266. ___   have the right to serve the mission of the church as a member without special obligations or privileges.

258. ___ 267. ___   develop a life based on personal goals and talents even if this prevents participation in the church.

259. ___ 268. ___   actively take part in decision making within the church even when that involves disagreement with her or his spouse.

260. ___ 269. ___   actively take part in decision making within the church even when that involves disagreement with other lay persons.

J. 270. Any comments you have regarding your perception of the present health/unhealth of the parish ministry, and any suggestions for improving it?

APPENDIX B

Life-styles and Heart Attacks:
A Supplement to Chapter 4

Two groups of clergy were compared across all survey items. The groups were those who answered "strongly agree" or "agree" (but not "tend to agree") versus those who answered "strongly disagree" or "disagree" (but not "tend to disagree") to item 189, "My life-style makes me a high risk for a heart attack."

The intent first of all was to see if the life-styles of the two groups differed noticeably. However, there were very few items that could really be used as definite indicators of differences in life-style. Most of the survey items allowed people to describe their perceptions of, opinions about, or attitudes toward certain aspects of their lives, but not to describe their behavior itself.

Strictly in terms of behavior, therefore, the two groups were found to differ in only ten respects. Those were principally concerning marital and family conflict, use of alcohol, and response to conflict and strong emotion, as follows:

More frequent response of *those seeing selves at risk*	Issue	More frequent response of *those not seeing selves at risk*
Frequently	Cannot communicate with spouse or quarrel constructively	Never
Frequently	Cannot cope with own children	Never
Frequently or occasionally	Self-sabotaging behavior, excessive use of alcohol or drugs, and drinking may become a problem	Never
Strongly agree	Tend to put off dealing with irritation/conflict	Disagree
Very Bothered	Tend to stuff own feelings	Little concern
Tend to disagree, disagree, or strongly disagree	Can say no to others and put own needs first without feeling guilty	Tend to agree, agree, or strongly agree
Tend to agree, agree, or strongly agree	Cannot live up to standards one sets for self	Tend to disagree, disagree, or strongly disagree

These differences are fundamental to the way people function psychologically and in their behavior.

The two groups do *not* differ significantly by gender, stage in family life, church body, ministerial position (e.g., senior pastor, solo pastor, chaplain, educator, etc.), whether serving one or more congregations or an institution, in the U.S. or other country, or in an urban or rural location. They also do *not* differ concerning the years of their ministries in which they experienced most stress, or in what they feel would improve the lot of clergy in general. Unfortunately there was no evidence whether they differ by size of the parishes they are serving.

However, there was evidence that *they do differ greatly* in almost all of the same ways that those dissatisfied with their spiritual/devotional lives differ from those who are not. *Those who perceive themselves to be at risk of a heart attack have much the same profile as the dissatisfied.*

Ways That Those Dissatisfied and Satisfied with Their Spiritual/Devotional Lives Differed in Which Those Who Perceive Themselves at Risk and Not at Risk of a Heart Attack Did Not Differ

1. Stage in family life, and type of ministry being performed
2. Average rating of the following aspects of their own ministries:
   - preaching
   - prophetic witness, youth work, work with the aging, evangelism, and sick visitation
3. The following potential sources of satisfaction:
   - personal accomplishment, and doing something of value
   - support from the congregation, respect and status in the community, and recognition by officers of congregation and district
4. Reasons for any dissatisfactions
5. The following potential sources of stress:
   - lack of employment for spouse
   - conflicts with one's own children
6. Frequency of giving one's family "the silent treatment"
7. The following recommendations to improve the lot of clergy:
   - retreats, workshops, and counseling for clergy and their families
   - training for Ministerial Relations committees
8. Agreement with the following ideas concerning roles of women:
   - that women's careers should be second
   - that spouses should always be supportive of clergy's ministry
   - that husbands and wives should share responsibility for household tasks
9. Degree of difficulty speaking out on social issues, and conviction that one could serve God better outside the ministry.

Ways That Those at Risk and Not at Risk of a Heart Attack Differed in Which Those Dissatisfied and Satisfied with Their Spiritual/ Devotional Lives Did Not Differ

More frequent response of those who *perceive themselves at risk*	Issue	More frequent response of those *not seeing themselves at risk*
Very unsatisfactory to unsure	Overall relationship with the congregation and with one's spouse	Very satisfactory
Somewhat to very serious stress	Community pressure on one's children; spouse regarded as extension of the pastor; conflict with the congregation; other clergy's jealousy; and physical health problems	No stress
Strongly agree or agree	Anxiety before and after difficult or hectic days; not enough financial security for retirement; I am getting old	Strongly disagree or disagree
Strongly agree	Society values success more than service	Tend to agree
Strongly agree or agree	Church values success like society does	Disagree or tend to disagree
Strongly agree, agree, or tend to agree	People who know me well feel I take my work too seriously; I get into moods where I can't seem to cheer up	Strongly disagree or disagree
Strongly agree, agree, tend to agree, or tend to disagree	I don't have enough money to make ends meet	Disagree

The general pattern of difference in degree of personal concern was for those at risk more frequently to be somewhat to very bothered over the issues mentioned in the last five paragraphs, while those who did not see themselves at risk more frequently reported never being bothered, no longer, or little bothered.

The differences between the two groups are reminiscent of the history of the measurement of stress. First attempts to measure stress were attempts to identify the numbers and kinds of negative or potentially stress-producing events in a person's recent experience. It was then discovered that the consequences of stress did not seem to vary in people's lives depending upon the numbers and kinds of negative events. Stress was found not to be a matter of the amount of potentially stress-producing experience, but of how the person responded to, felt about, interpreted, and gave meaning to those negative events. The same may be the case here. We do not have the evidence we need in order to know whether the life-styles of the two groups do actually differ that much. We do know that those who perceive themselves at risk are more dissatisfied, anxious, depressed, in conflict, afraid of conflict, serious, worried, aware of stress and pressure, and bothered by their condition. Therefore, the message of Chapter 4 about acceptance of grace and limits is particularly applicable to them.

We also know that they resemble not only the "hurting" but more so those dissatisfied with their spiritual/devotional lives. Therefore, the counsel offered in Chapter 2 is also applicable to them.

APPENDIX C

Distribution of Functions
in Living Units

Below is a listing of various activities that take place in a living unit (a couple, or a group of people living together). The way they get done varies a great deal from unit to unit but they do tend to change over the unit life cycle. Please indicate in the appropriate column:

1. by whom the activity is now done, with a ✔ (*check mark*).
2. by whom this activity would *ideally* be done, with an * (asterisk).

Write in additional items that are omitted but you judge important.

	Mutually Shared	Woman Primarily	Woman Exclusively	Man Primarily	Man Exclusively
1. Clean, dust, pick up					
2. Vacuum					
3. Toilets/bathrooms					
4. Scrub floors					
5. Make beds					
6. Iron					
7. Laundry					
8. Water houseplants					

185

	Mutually Shared	Woman Primarily	Woman Exclusively	Man Primarily	Man Exclusively
9. Clean stove and oven					
10. Wash windows					
11. Dust and clean furniture					
12. Build fire					
13. Clean fireplace					
14. Pack lunches					
15. Cook dinner					
16. Make breakfast					
17. Plan meals					
18. Wash dishes					
19. Clean up kitchen					
20. Barbeque					
21. Bake					
22.					
23.					
24. Garden					
25. Lawn and plants					
26. Shovel snow					
27. Pet care					
28. Garbage					
29.					
30.					
31. Discipline children					
32. Attend school functions					
33. Sex education					
34. Family devotions					
35. Children to bed					
36. Children when sick					
37. Children's vocation					
38.					
39.					
40. Major purchases					

	Mutually Shared	Woman Primarily	Woman Exclusively	Man Primarily	Man Exclusively
41. Minor purchases					
42. Purchase gifts					
43.					
44.					
45. Do income tax					
46. Earn income					
47. Manage investments					
48. Purchase stocks					
49. Make budget					
50. Error in credit cards					
51. Banking					
52. Pay bills					
53. Keep accounts					
54. Reconcile checkbook					
55. Clip coupons					
56. Pay babysitter					
57.					
58.					
59. Christmas cards					
60. Thank you notes					
61. Invite people for meals					
62. Secure babysitter					
63. Plan recreation					
64. Secure tickets					
65. Make reservations					
66. Shop for food					
67. Plan vacations					
68. Arrange flights, hotels					
69. Clothes to cleaners					
70.					
71.					
72.					

	Mutually Shared	Woman Primarily	Woman Exclusively	Man Primarily	Man Exclusively
73. Wallpaper					
74. Electrical repair					
75. Plumbing repair					
76. Paint interior					
77. Light carpentry					
78. Paint exterior					
79. Clean garage					
80. Clean work area					
81.					
82.					
83.					
84. Gas car					
85. Car repairs					
86. Car maintenance					
87. Wash car					
88. Drive car for couple					
89. Change tires					
90. Buy car					
91.					
92.					

✔ and * totals

NOTES

Introduction

1. David Schuller, Merton Strommen, and Milo Brekke, eds., *Ministry in America* (San Francisco: Harper & Row, 1978); Merton Strommen et al., *A Study of Generations* (Minneapolis: Augsburg Publishing House, 1972).

Chapter 1

1. Thomas E. Kadel, ed., *Growth in Ministry* (Philadelphia: Fortress, 1980).
2. *Congregational Life Dynamics,* Exhibit D-49, Addendum D.
3. *Sickness unto Death* (Princeton: Princeton University Press, 1954), p. 218.
4. "On Communications—Interview with Howard Anderson," *Computerworld,* March 14, 1982, vol. 18, no. 11A.
5. *Congregational Life Dynamics,* p. 8; Exhibit D, p. 48.

Chapter 2

1. *Ministry with the Aging* (San Francisco: Harper & Row, 1983), p. 96.
2. *Minister as Diagnostician* (Philadelphia: Westminster, 1976), p. 47.
3. T. Kadel, ed., *Growth in Ministry* (Philadelphia: Fortress, 1980).
4. Typical of which is *Reaching Out* (Garden City, N.Y.: Doubleday and Co., 1975).
5. *Celebration of Discipline* (San Francisco: Harper & Row, 1978).

Chapter 3

1. Thomas J. Peters and Robert H. Waterman Jr., *In Search of Excellence* (New York: Warner, 1984).

Chapter 4

1. M. Scott Peck, *People of the Lie* (New York: Simon and Schuster, 1983).
2. Søren Kierkegaard, *Sickness unto Death* (Princeton: Princeton University Press, 1954), p. 220.
3. *Feed My Sheep* (New York: Paulist Press, 1984), p. 147.
4. Thomas J. Peters and Robert H. Waterman Jr., *In Search of Excellence* (New York: Warner, 1984).
5. Ibid., p. 269.
6. Charlie Shedd, *Letters to Karen* (New York: Avon, 1968), p. 44.

Chapter 5

1. Books helpful in the management of conflict include the following: C. Douglas Lewis, *Resolving Church Conflicts* (New York: Harper & Row, 1981); David Augsburger, *Caring Enough to Confront,* rev. ed. (Scottdale, Pa.: Herald Press, 1980); James E. Dittes, *When the People Say No* (New York: Harper & Row, 1979); Paul Kittlaus and Speed Leas, *Church Fights* (Philadelphia: Westminster, 1973); Roger Fisher and William Ury, *Getting to Yes* (New York: Penguin, 1973).
2. *Conflict Management,* audio cassette.
3. Center for Application of Psychological Type, P.O. Box 13807, University Station, Gainesville, FL 32604.
4. Roy M. Oswald, *Crossing the Boundary* (Washington, D.C.: Alban Institute, 1980).

Chapter 6

1. Frederick Herzberg, *Work and the Nature of Man* (Cleveland: World, 1966).

Chapter 7

1. *The Road Less Traveled* (New York: Simon and Schuster, 1978), pp. 68-69.